Over-the-Counter Derivatives Regulation in Hong Kong and Singapore

Over-the-Counter Derivatives Regulation in Hong Kong and Singapore

By

Christopher Chen

BRILL

LEIDEN | BOSTON

Library of Congress Control Number: 2016962783

Typeface for the Latin, Greek, and Cyrillic scripts: "Brill". See and download: brill.com/brill-typeface.

ISBN 978-90-04-34339-9 (paperback)
ISBN 978-90-04-34341-2 (e-book)

Originally published as Volume 1(4) 2016, in *International Banking and Securities Law*,
DOI 10.1163/24056936-12340004

Copyright 2017 by Christopher Chen. Published by Koninklijke Brill NV, Leiden, The Netherlands.
Koninklijke Brill NV incorporates the imprints Brill, Brill Hes & De Graaf, Brill Nijhoff, Brill Rodopi and Hotei Publishing.
Koninklijke Brill NV reserves the right to protect the publication against unauthorized use and to authorize dissemination by means of offprints, legitimate photocopies, microform editions, reprints, translations, and secondary information sources, such as abstracting and indexing services including databases. Requests for commercial re-use, use of parts of the publication, and/or translations must be addressed to Koninklijke Brill NV.

This book is printed on acid-free paper and produced in a sustainable manner.

Contents

List of Acronyms VII

Over-the-Counter Derivatives Regulation in Hong Kong and Singapore 1
    Christopher Chen
  Abstract 1
  Keywords 1
  Introduction 1
  1 Transnational OTC Derivatives Regulations 4
    1.1 *Regulatory Background* 4
    1.2 *The Adoption of ISDA Master Agreement in the Practice* 8
  2 Regulatory Scope: General Definition of Derivatives 10
    2.1 *Singapore* 10
    2.2 *Hong Kong* 12
    2.3 *Summary* 13
  3 The Reporting Mandate 14
    3.1 *General Introduction* 14
    3.2 *Legal Mandate and Jurisdiction Scope* 15
    3.3 *Who—Reporting Parties* 17
        3.3.1 Singapore 18
        3.3.2 Hong Kong 19
        3.3.3 Comparison 21
    3.4 *What—Reportable Transactions* 21
    3.5 *Compliance Issues* 23
        3.5.1 Timing and Back-loading 23
        3.5.2 How to Report: Single-sided or Dual Reporting 24
        3.5.3 Information to be Reported 25
        3.5.4 Report to Whom and Substituted Compliance 26
  4 Clearing Mandate 27
    4.1 *General Introduction* 27
    4.2 *Legal Mandate and Jurisdiction Scope* 30
    4.3 *Who—Clearing Parties and Clearing Threshold* 32
    4.4 *Transactions Subject to the Clearing Obligation and Exempted Transactions* 35
        4.4.1 General 35
        4.4.2 Hedging or End-user Exemption 36
        4.4.3 Intragroup or Affiliate Exemptions 37
        4.4.4 Other Exemptions 39

    4.5 *Some Compliance Issues* 40
          4.5.1   Timing and Back-loading 40
          4.5.2   Substituted Compliance 40
          4.5.3   Documentation Issues 42
5 The Trading Mandate 42
6 Convergence, Divergence or a Room for Arbitrage? An Evaluation of Positions in Hong Kong and Singapore 45
7 Conclusions 47
    Bibliography 47

List of Acronyms

BCBS	Basel Committee on Banking Supervision
BIS	Bank of International Settlement
CCP	Central counterparty
CDS	Credit default swaps
CFTC	Commodity Futures Trading Commission
DFA	Dodd-Frank Wall Street Reform and Consumer Protection Act
EMIR	European Market Infrastructure Regulation
ESMA	European Securities and Markets Authority
EU	European Union
FSB	Financial Stability Board
HKEx	Hong Kong Exchange
HKMA	Hong Kong Monetary Authority
HKSFC	Hong Kong Securities and Futures Commission
IRS	Interest rate swaps
ISDA	International Swaps and Derivatives Association
MAS	Monetary Authority of Singapore
OTC	Over the counter
TR	Trade repository
SFA	Securities and Futures Act (Cap 289), Singapore
SFO	Securities and Futures Ordinance (Cap 571), Hong Kong

Over-the-Counter Derivatives Regulation in Hong Kong and Singapore

Christopher Chen
Singapore Management University
chchen@smu.edu.sg

Abstract

In this article, Dr Christopher Chen examines and compares the regulation of over-the-counter derivatives in Hong Kong and Singapore, the two largest international financial centres in Asia Pacific. Dr Chen analyses current or proposed regulations on trade reporting, centralised clearing and mandatory exchange trading mandates regarding OTC derivatives against the backdrop of reforms of international financial regulatory structure after the global financial crisis. The article also relates the reforms in Asia to development in major Western markets such as the U.S., U.K. or European Union. Apart from technical comparison and dissecting of content of rules from different angles, this article also examines the rationale behind those reforms and policy concerns behind Asian adoption of the regulatory mandates prescribed by G20 as well as potential policy concerns (such as competition and extraterritoriality) in a market that is dominated by Western banks.

Keywords

derivatives – financial regulation – Singapore – Hong Kong – trade reporting – centralised clearing – CCP – exchange trading – substituted compliance

Introduction

This article examines the regulation of over-the-counter (OTC) derivatives in Singapore and Hong Kong, the two largest international financial centres in

---

* The author thanks the referees for their useful and constructive comments.

Asia Pacific, against the globalisation of the derivatives market and financial regulatory reforms since the global financial crisis in an area dominated by U.S. and European markets. We also reflect upon the current state of developments in the two city-states in the context of national competition in the changing landscape of the global financial market.

The market of OTC derivatives is a trillion-dollar business. According to data released by the Bank of International Settlement (BIS) in 2016, total open interests in all exchange-traded contracts reached U.S.$24.69 trillion in December 2015, and the total notional amount of OTC derivatives amounted to U.S.$552.91 trillion in the first half of 2015. The market is also global in nature, with a wide range of underlying assets traded in different parts of the world (e.g., the MSCI China Index futures traded in Singapore). Some exchange-traded products also serve as global benchmarks to set the price for wholesale or consumable items around the world (e.g., the West Texas Intermediate Futures traded in the New York Mercantile Exchange).

However, the market also has two clear centres of power: the United Kingdom (U.K.) and the United States (U.S.). According the Triennial Central Bank Survey published by the BIS in 2013,[1] the U.K. led the daily average of OTC interest rate derivatives with U.S.$1347.75 billion, followed by the U.S. (628.15 billion), France (202.21 billion) and Germany (101.34 billion). Asian markets lagged behind, with Japan being the largest (67.14 billion, fifth in the world), followed closely by Australia (66.18 billion, sixth). The two largest financial centres in Asia-Pacific outside Japan fell further behind, with Singapore (37.14 billion) in eighth and Hong Kong (27.90 billion) in twelfth. Despite its huge economy, China's OTC derivatives market is negligible (12.966 billion in 2013).[2] According to the same survey in April 2016, the U.S. led with U.S.$1,241 billion (for daily average of all interest rate derivatives) followed by the U.K. (1,180 billion) and France (141 billion), while Hong Kong (141 billion) and Singapore (58 billion) jumped ahead of Japan (56 billion) and Australia (49 billion) in the global league table.[3] This shows a trend of Hong Kong and Singapore rising as trading centres of OTC derivatives in Asia Pacific.

---

1 Bank of International Settlement, 'Triennial Central Bank Survey: Interest Rate Derivatives Market Turnover in 2013' (2013) at 1, in http://www.bis.org/publ/rpfx13.htm.
2 *Id.*, at 8.
3 Bank of International Settlement, 'Triennial Central Bank Survey of foreign exchange and OTC derivatives markets in 2016' in http://www.bis.org/publ/rpfx16.htm. See in particular Table D12.1 in http://stats.bis.org/statx/srs/table/d12.1.

For a long while, the market of OTC derivatives was seen as a 'no man's land',[4] as the market seemed to be situated between several regulatory systems without a dedicated and comprehensive set of regulations. Private ordering was the main tool to regulate the fast-growing OTC derivatives market before the financial crisis.[5] The collapse of Lehman Brothers in September 2008 and the global financial crisis changed the scene. Seen as one of the main culprits of the global crisis,[6] we have seen major regulatory reforms regarding OTC derivatives since then. In 2009 at the Pittsburgh Summit, the G20 declared a commitment to strengthening the international financial regulatory system. In particular, the G20 suggested that '[a]ll standardized OTC derivative contracts should be traded on exchanges or electronic trading platforms...and cleared through central counterparties by end-2012 at the latest'.[7] Moreover, 'OTC derivative contracts should be reported to trade repositories';[8] otherwise they 'should be subject to higher capital requirements'.[9] Based on this statement, there are three main regulatory mandates regarding OTC derivatives: the reporting mandate, the clearing mandate and the trading mandate. The purpose of those mandates is to control counterparty risk, to improve transparency and to prevent systemic risk via the derivatives market.

This article will approach the regulation of OTC derivatives in Singapore and Hong Kong from several dimensions. We begin by considering the motives and intentions of Singapore and Hong Kong to implement the three mandates regarding OTC derivatives in their much smaller markets, which sets the backdrop and benchmarks for our examination of regulatory developments in the two city-states. We then consider in more detail the issues linked to documentation and definitions of OTC derivatives before a thorough discussion of the rules regarding the reporting, clearing and trading mandates. We compare rules in Singapore and Hong Kong as in December 2016 and connect local developments to those in the U.S. and Europe to present a global picture. We deconstruct some of the three mandates into several elements, including legal sources, the persons who are obliged by a mandate, the types of derivatives

---

4 Cohen S. S., 'Financial Services Regulation: A Mid-Decade Review: Colloquium: The Challenge of Derivatives' (1995) 63 *Fordham Law Review* 1993, 2013.
5 See generally Awrey D., 'The Dynamics of OTC Derivatives Regulation: Bridging the Public-Private Divide' (2010) 11 *European Business Organization Law Review* 155.
6 Avgouleas E., *Governance of Global Financial Markets: The Law, The Economics, The Politics* 96–97 (Cambridge University Press 2012).
7 G20, *Leaders' Statement—The Pittsburgh Summit*, at 11, https://g20.org/wp-content/uploads/2014/12/Pittsburgh_Declaration_0.pdf.
8 *Id.*
9 *Id.*

that are subject to the mandate(s), exemptions and exceptions, substituted compliance, back-loading and some compliance issues to offer a more systematic examination and comparison of national rules before we conclude with an overall evaluation. A list of acronyms is provide at the end of the paper.

1   Transnational OTC Derivatives Regulations

1.1   *Regulatory Background*

Broadly, we may view the implementation process of OTC derivatives regulation in Asia against international law-making and standard-setting in the financial sector. On the one hand, the process is partly a reaction to global pressure on international centres such as Singapore and Hong Kong and their engagement in global rule-making. On the other hand, the manner in which regulations are developed also reflects some (sometimes conflicting) domestic interests such as the need to maintain the soundness of the local financial market and the desire for greater competition in business.

On the international level, OTC derivatives regulations were developed via the so-called 'soft law' approach. Instead of an international treaty (i.e., 'hard law') regulating international finance (as in the case of international trade and the World Trade Organisation), international financial regulatory actions since the global financial crisis have relied on agreements between politicians or regulators amongst two or more states that provide substantive commitments that the parties are expected to take seriously.[10] In the case of international financial regulations, those commitments were developed via 'transnational regulatory networks' (TRNs) whereby the 'drafters of [international standards] are informal committees of ministry officials, regulators, or private experts.'[11] Participating countries in a TRN are expected to follow the standards, thereby effectively making the standards a kind of 'international law' without a treaty. The most prominent example of this approach is the Basel Accord on the capital adequacy of banks published by the Basel Committee on Banking Supervision (BCBS) under the BIS. Members of the BCBS include central banks and financial regulators of 28 markets, including Hong Kong and Singapore. After the global financial crisis, it remains the main vehicle for making international rulings. The Financial Stability Board (FSB) has published

---

10   Galbraith J. and Zaring D., 'Soft Law as Foreign Relations Law' (2014) 99 *Cornell Law Review* 735, 739–740.
11   Gadinis S., 'Three Pathways to Global Standards: Private, Regulator, and Ministry Network' (2015) 109 *American Journal of International Law* 1, 1.

some standards in an attempt to harmonise the resolution regimes of international financial institutions worldwide.[12] The soft law approach may partly reflect regulators' desire for speed, flexibility and expertise[13] and their desire to avoid the sometimes treacherous process of treaty-making, which might lead to limited or failed international cooperation.[14] The soft law approach also reflects the importance of cross-border regulatory cooperation in ensuring financial stability.[15]

International regulations on OTC derivatives also fall into the same pattern. As mentioned earlier, it was first declared by the G20 as the key agenda for reform in the area. It was then picked up by the FSB and major financial markets. However, in the case of OTC derivatives, the FSB did not create substantive standards like the Basel Accord. Instead, the FSB only made some initial recommendations regarding standardisation of the market, central clearing, trading platforms and reporting to trade repositories.[16] The FSB only monitors the implementation process of its member states with periodical progress reports every six months.

Singapore and Hong Kong are both members of major TRNs such as the FSB, BIS, BCBS, International Organisation of Securities Commissions and International Association of Insurance Supervisors, although neither is a member of G20 or the Organisation of Economic Cooperation and Development. This presents an interesting situation. Neither has direct influence on the global political arena at the top level.[17] Nonetheless, both actively participate in global standards-making via those TRNs, which reflects the status of Singapore and Hong Kong as top-tier financial centres.

On the national level, various domestic and policy concerns face politicians and technocrats in each state. First, there are economic factors. Because both Singapore and Hong Kong thrive as global trading hubs and international

---

12 Financial Stability Board, 'Key Attributes of Effective Resolution Regimes for Financial Institutions' (2014), http://www.fsb.org/wp-content/uploads/r_111104cc.pdf?page_moved=1.
13 Verdier P.-H., 'The Political Economy of International Financial Regulation' (2013) 88 *Indiana Law Journal* 1405, 1456–1459.
14 Cho S. and Kelly C. R., 'Promises and Perils of New Global Governance: A Case of the G20' (2012) 12 *Chicago Journal International Law* 491, 497–498.
15 Brummer C., *Soft Law and the Global Financial System: Rule Making in the 21st Century* 16 (Cambridge University Press 2012).
16 Financial Stability Board, *Implementing OTC Derivatives Market Reforms* (2010), http://www.financialstabilityboard.org/wp-content/uploads/r_101025.pdf.
17 However, Hong Kong, as a special district under Chinese rule, might tap in the presence of China.

financial centres, it is natural that both city-states would attempt to keep up with international developments to compete for larger market shares in the global derivatives market. In Singapore, it is enshrined in legislation; the Monetary Authority of Singapore Act makes it clear that one of the principal objects and functions of the Monetary Authority of Singapore (MAS) is to foster Singapore's growth as an internationally competitive financial centre.[18] In Hong Kong, the Basic Law prescribes that '[t]he Government of the Hong Kong Special Administrative Region shall provide an appropriate economic and legal environment for the maintenance of the status of Hong Kong as an international financial centre'.[19] Therefore, both city-states have solid legal mandates to compete to maintain their status as international financial centres. Such a desire may affect their interests in adopting international standards to attract participants from foreign markets.

However, the desire to compete does not necessarily mean there will be a race to the bottom. It is of utmost importance to maintain the soundness of the market. In Singapore, one of the missions of financial regulators is to foster a sound and reputable financial centre.[20] In Hong Kong, '[t]he principal function of the Monetary Authority under this Ordinance shall be to promote the general stability and effective working of the banking system.'[21] Neither market would remain a financial centre without a solid and healthy financial market.

For this purpose, both Singapore and Hong Kong must ensure that their financial infrastructure and financial institutions are resilient and remain solvent. For example, as discussed below, one of the conditions to successful centralised clearing is to ensure the solvency and safety of the clearing service provider.[22] Therefore, if a certain action would endanger the soundness of the domestic financial market, regulators might be less willing to adopt it to avoid backlash in the domestic financial market and to avoid global pressure, even if the action may help to gain some more businesses in the short term. This offers a natural restraint on concerns of racing to the bottom.

In addition, we observe that both markets adopt a wait-and-see approach. Instead of making regulations upon G20's mandate, both markets begin to develop regulations after the U.S. and the European Union (EU). In the leading markets, the U.S. passed the Dodd-Frank Wall Street Reform and Consumer

---

18 Monetary Authority of Singapore Act (Cap 186, Revised Edition 1999) s 4(1)(d) (Singapore).
19 Hong Kong Basic Law article 109.
20 Monetary Authority of Singapore Act s 4(1)(b) (Singapore).
21 Banking Ordinance (Cap 155, Revised Edition 2008) s 7(1) (Hong Kong). See also Securities and Futures Ordinance (Cap 571) s 5(1) (Hong Kong).
22 See below Part VI.

Protection Act (DFA) in 2010,[23] with many subsidiary regulations issued by the Commodity Futures Trading Commission (CFTC) and the Securities Exchange Commission.[24] In Europe, the EU enacted the European Market Infrastructure Regulations (EMIR) in 2012,[25] with further regulations issued by the EU or the European Securities and Markets Authority (ESMA).[26]

In the Far East, Japan has been the most active player in compliance with the G20 proposal to reform its regulations on OTC derivatives. In the FSB's first progress report dated April 2011, only the U.S. and Japan had enacted legislation to implement the reforms.[27] Hong Kong and Singapore remain behind in its implementation. In Singapore, the MAS published its first consultation on derivatives regulation only in February 2012,[28] followed by further consultation in May 2012.[29] The Securities and Futures Act (SFA) was amended in 2012 to impose reporting and clearing mandates.[30] The reporting mandate came into force on 11 November 2014,[31] and the implementation of the clearing mandate is likely to take place in the second half of 2016.[32] The MAS was only

---

23 Pub Law 111–203 (2010). (DFA).
24 For a list of rules made by the Commodity Futures Trading Commission (CFTC) following the DFA, see the CFTC's website: http://www.cftc.gov/LawRegulation/DoddFrankAct/index.htm.
25 Regulation (E.U.) No. 648/2012 of the European Parliament and of the Council of 4 July 2012 on OTC derivatives, central counterparties and trade repositories.
26 For European regulations, see the EU's website: http://ec.europa.eu/finance/financial-markets/derivatives/index_en.htm.
27 Financial Stability Board, OTC *Derivatives Market Reforms—Progress Report on Implementation*, at 8, http://www.financialstabilityboard.org/wp-content/uploads/r_110415b.pdf.
28 Monetary Authority of Singapore, *Proposed Regulation of OTC Derivatives* (Consultation Paper P003–2012, 2012), http://www.mas.gov.sg/News-and-Publications/Consultation-Paper/2012/Consultation-Paper-on-Proposed-Regulation-of-OTC-Derivatives.aspx.
29 Monetary Authority of Singapore, *Consultation Paper I on Proposed Amendments to the Securities and Futures Act on Regulation of OTC Derivatives* (Consultation Paper P008–2012, 2012), http://www.mas.gov.sg/News-and-Publications/Consultation-Paper/2012/Consultation-Paper-I-on-Proposed-Amendments-to-the-SFA-on-Regulation-of-OTC-Derivatives.aspx.
30 Securities and Futures (Amendment) Act 2012 (Act 34 of 2012) s 27 (Singapore). (SFA).
31 Securities and Futures (Reporting of Derivatives Contracts) Regulation 2013 (S 727/2014) (Singapore). (Singapore Reporting Rules).
32 MAS, *Draft Regulations for Mandatory Clearing of Derivatives Contracts* (Consultation Paper P010–2015, 2015), http://www.mas.gov.sg/News-and-Publications/Consultation-Paper/2015/Consultation-Paper-on-Draft-Regulations-for-Mandatory-Clearing-of-Derivatives-Contracts.aspx.

considering imposition of the trading mandate in the SFA in February 2015.[33] In Hong Kong, regulators published the first consultation paper in October 2011,[34] with conclusions published in July 2012[35] before further consultation starting in July 2012.[36] The Securities and Futures Ordinance (SFO) was amended in March 2014 to impose the clearing, reporting and trading mandates for OTC derivative transactions, although only the reporting mandate has been fully implemented as of May 2016.

In other words, regulators in both Hong Kong and Singapore monitored the developments in bigger markets. For example, Hong Kong's first consultation paper tracked implementation efforts not only in the U.S. and the EU, but also in Japan, Australia and Singapore.[37] In Singapore, the MAS constantly modelled its proposals on the positions taken by the U.S. and the EU.[38] Therefore, Hong Kong and Singapore waited for European regulations to be largely set before they began to remake their own local rules. Those pave the ground for the establishment of OTC derivatives regulations in Singapore and Hong Kong.

1.2   *The Adoption of ISDA Master Agreement in the Practice*

Before we explore the details of OTC derivatives regulations in Singapore and Hong Kong since the global financial crisis, it worthwhile to consider briefly the adoption of international standard forms in both markets. In the past 30 years, a phenomenon unseen in other areas of finance is the widespread use of the master agreement published by the International Swaps and Derivatives

---

33   Monetary Authority of Singapore, 'Consultation Paper on Proposed Amendments to the Securities and Futures Act (P004–2015)', http://www.mas.gov.sg/News-and-Publications/Consultation-Paper/2015/Consultation-Paper-on-Proposed-Amendments-to-the-SFA.aspx.

34   Hong Kong Securities and Futures Commission, *Consultation Paper on the Proposed Regulatory Regime for the Over-the-Counter Derivatives Market in Hong Kong* (2011), http://www.sfc.hk/edistributionWeb/gateway/EN/consultation/doc?refNo=11CP6.

35   Hong Kong Securities and Futures Commission, *Joint Consultation Conclusions on the Proposed Regulatory Regime for the Over-the-counter Derivatives Market in Hong Kong* (2012), http://www.sfc.hk/edistributionWeb/gateway/EN/consultation/conclusion?refNo=11CP6.

36   Hong Kong Securities and Futures Commission, *Supplement Consultation on the OTC Derivatives Regime for Hong Kong – Proposed Scope of New/Expanded Regulated Activities and Regulatory Oversight of Systemically Important Players* (2012), http://www.sfc.hk/edistributionWeb/gateway/EN/consultation/doc?refNo=12CP2.

37   Above note 34, Appendix A.

38   Above note 28.

Association (ISDA; i.e., the ISDA form).[39] Although no official data exist, one estimates that about 90% of the global OTC derivatives transactions adopt one of the ISDA forms.[40] Literally, the ISDA form has become the one and only 'transnational business governance regime' for the global OTC derivatives market.

Headquartered in New York City, the ISDA was initially a trade association to represent the interests of major dealers (i.e., large banks in the U.S., U.K. and Europe). It was natural that the primary governing law of the ISDA forms (in both the 1992 and the 2002 editions) was established as either New York or English law, with disputes governed by New York or English courts.[41] This features make it easier for either Singapore or Hong Kong to adopt the ISDA form in practice. As former British colonies, Singapore and Hong Kong both inherited the English legal system. The entire private law and commercial law system is quite similar to that in England.[42] Therefore, legal practitioners and market participants have no difficulty adopting the ISDA form.

In academic terms, both markets are more 'fitting' to import the norms created by the ISDA form.[43] Moreover, because both Singapore and Hong Kong are open economies that strive for trading and finance, acceptance of the standard form used in major markets in the West helps to develop the local market. After all, if large Western banks (which are likely to be counterparties to a local financial institution or a non-financial firm) decide to use the ISDA form, local parties may have no choice but to accept the ISDA Master Agreement. Whilst the MAS in Singapore has not officially done so in any regulation, the Hong Kong Monetary Authority expressly recognises that 'market participants have increasingly seen the advantage of adopting a consistent approach to deal with

---

39 For more background on the rise of the ISDA form, see generally Flanagan S. M., 'The Rise of a Trade Association: Group Interactions within the International Swaps and Derivatives Association' (2001) 6 *Harvard Negotiation Law Review* 211.

40 Henderson S. K., *Henderson on Derivatives* 803 (2nd Ed, LexisNexis 2010).

41 1992 or 2002 ISDA Master Agreement section 13 and Schedule Part 4(h).

42 For a discussion on Singapore's commercial law, see generally Chen C., 'Measuring the Transplantation of English Commercial Law in a Small Jurisdiction: An Empirical Study of Singapore's Insurance Judgments between 1965 and 2012' (2014) 49 *Texas International Law Journal* 469, 475–482.

43 Kanda H. and Milhaupt C. J., 'Re-Examining Legal Transplants: The Director's Fiduciary Duty in Japanese Corporate Law' (2003) 51 *American Journal of Comparative Law* 887, 891.

the issue, e.g., using the standard clauses prepared by the International Swaps and Derivatives Association'.[44]

The seamless adoption of the ISDA form paved a solid path for the development of the derivatives markets in Singapore and Hong Kong, further supporting their position as Asian's international financial centres. This also helped local market participants to connect with major global players. In turn, this may make the adoption and implementation of the regulatory mandates related to OTC derivatives slightly easier, at least from a transactional front.

2 Regulatory Scope: General Definition of Derivatives

The first step toward regulation is usually to define OTC derivatives, the subject-matter of regulation, in legal terms. In general, a derivative is a financial instrument whose value depends upon another underlying variable. However, this general definition may not be sufficiently precise to be deemed a legal definition. As a matter of fact, the value of most (if not all) financial instruments (e.g., a stock) depends upon a wide range of factors (e.g., economic factors or general market movements), which increases the difficulty of establishing a definite definition. In fact, lawmakers have defined the term in a variety of ways, and we have found no universal definition of the term, exemplified by Singapore's and Hong Kong's definitions.[45]

2.1 *Singapore*

Singapore takes a different approach within the framework of the SFA. The 2012 amendment of the Act inserts some new terms into the Act alongside existing categories of 'futures' (which capture exchange-traded contracts) and 'leveraged foreign exchange trading' to deal with OTC derivatives. First, on the general level, the term 'derivatives contract' is defined as a forward contract, an option contract, a swap contract or any contract or transaction that is prescribed by the MAS by regulations, with the exception of securities or futures contracts or those otherwise exempted by the MAS. This defines the outer

---

44 Hong Kong Monetary Authority Guideline No. 7.6 (2012), http://www.hkma.gov.hk/eng/key-information/guidelines-and-circulars/guidelines/guide_76b.shtml.

45 See 7 USC 1a(47) for definition under the Dodd-Frank Act in the U.S. For definitions under EU law, see European Market Infrastructure Regulation (Regulations No 648/2012, EMIR) art 2(5), referring to points (4) to (10) of Section C of Annex I to Derivative 2004/39/EC.

scope of 'derivatives contract'.[46] Clearly, it does not include those instruments that are already defined as 'securities' and exchange-traded futures contracts.

Second, the terms 'forward contract', 'option contract' and 'swap contract' each have their own definition, each referring to an 'underlying thing'. For example, a forward contract generally means 'a contract under which one party agrees to transfer title ... or a specified quantity of a specified underlying thing to another party at a specified future time and at a specified price'.[47] The definition for an option contract is similar, except that it was structured as an option.[48] In addition, a swap contract means 'a contract for differences, or a contract the purpose or purported of which is to secure a profit or avoid a loss by reference to fluctuations in the value or price of one or more underlying things'.[49] The wordings seem to inherit the language in the definition of contract for differences under U.K. law.[50]

However, Singapore law uses 'purported purpose' instead of 'pretended purpose' as under the U.K. law. This article suggests that the differences in wordings should not substantially change the substance of the definitions. No case law exists in Singapore considering the exact meaning of contract for differences, so we may expect that English cases may be helpful to determine the scope of 'swap contract' when it comes to the meaning of 'securing a profit'.[51]

Regardless of the kind of derivatives contract, it must refer to an 'underlying thing', which is defined to include a commodity, the credit of any person or any arrangement that is prescribed by the MAS.[52] Two points are worth noting. On the one hand, 'commodity' is a generic term that covers gold, goods, financial instruments or indices or interest in such a commodity.[53] Although only 'gold' is specifically mentioned in addition to 'goods', agricultural products, other metals and energy should still come within the definition of commodity. The term 'financial instrument' includes 'any currency, currency index, interest rate, interest rate instrument, interest rate index, share, share index, stock, stock index, debenture, bond index, a group or groups of such financial

---

46 SFA s 2 (derivatives contract) (Singapore).
47 SFA s 2 (forward contract) (Singapore).
48 SFA s 2 (option contract) (Singapore).
49 SFA s 2 (swap contract) (Singapore).
50 Financial Services and Markets Act 2000 (2000 c.8) Schedule 2 paragraph 19 (U.K.). See also Financial Services and Markets Act 2000 (Regulated Activities) Order 2001 (SI 2001/554) article 85(1) (U.K.).
51 *City Index Ltd v Leslie* [1992] QB 98 (CA).
52 SFA s 2 (Singapore).
53 SFA s 2 (Singapore).

instruments, and any other thing that is prescribed by the [regulator].'[54] Thus, the definition of a 'commodity' under the SFA is sufficiently broad to cover most financial instruments or any index thereof.

On the other hand, the term 'the credit of any person' may cause some confusion. The target is clearly credit derivatives. However, Singapore's definition differs from that under U.K. and European law, which specifies 'derivative instruments for the transfer of credit risk'.[55] Potential meanings of the 'credit of any person' may range from credit events or the creditworthiness of a person to simply a line of credit or the credibility of a person. Moreover, if we combine the definition of swap contract with 'the credit of a person', it may cover credit insurance policies, which are governed by the Insurance Act.[56] This may require some clarification in the future should any legal dispute arise.

In sum, Singapore has adopted a descriptive way to define the scope of 'derivative contract'. In early 2015, the MAS proposed to overhaul the relevant definitions in the SFA, including securities, futures and derivatives contracts, to improve legal certainty.[57] However, as of mid-2016, it has not yet entered into the legislative process.

2.2 Hong Kong

Hong Kong's approach differs from Singapore. The 2014 amendment of the SFO in Hong Kong creates a general definition for 'OTC derivative product'.[58] The SFO defines an 'OTC derivative product' as a 'structured product'. This refers to an addition to the definition of 'structured product' in 2011.[59] However, there is a long list of instruments that do not come within the definition of an OTC derivative product. These instruments are illustrated below.

Under the SFO, a structured product is an instrument under which some or all of the return or amount due (or both the return and the amount due) or the method of settlement is determined by reference to one or more changes in price or value of any type (or combination or basket) of securities, commodity, index, property, interest rate, currency rate or futures contract, or by reference

---

54 *Id.*

55 MiFID, Annex I Section C, Point 8.

56 Cap 142, Revised Edition 2002.

57 Monetary Authority of Singapore, 'Consultation Paper on Proposed Amendments to the Securities and Futures Act (P004–2015)' at 3–4, http://www.mas.gov.sg/News-and-Publications/Consultation-Paper/2015/Consultation-Paper-on-Proposed-Amendments-to-the-SFA.aspx.

58 Securities and Futures Ordinance (Cap 571) Schedule 1 paragraph 1B (Hong Kong). (SFO).

59 SFO Schedule 1 paragraph 1A (Hong Kong).

to the occurrence or non-occurrence of any specified event.[60] However, the definition does not include convertible bonds, subscription warrants, collective investment schemes, depositary receipts, debentures with variable interest rates (with exceptions), instruments issued to bona fide employees or families, contracts of insurance or any instrument prescribed by the Hong Kong Securities and Futures Commission (HKSFC).[61]

The SFO also provides a specific definition for 'spot contract' to accommodate commercial contracts that are deliverable in the future. In short, a spot contract is a contract for the sale of any underlying assets 'under the terms of which the settlement of the contract is scheduled to be made within' two business days or a period generally accepted in the market for a particular type of asset (whichever is longer).[62]

Second, even if a derivative falls within the definition of a 'structured product', there are some exceptions. According to the SFO, an OTC derivative product does not include exchange-traded stocks or futures, a structured product authorised and offered to the public (i.e., issued to the general public), asset-backed securities, debentures or deposits with a feature embedded to make them structured products, spot contracts, standardised and short-term products (offered within two weeks) and those prescribed by the HKSFC.[63]

2.3 *Summary*

In sum, by comparing the definitions in Singapore and Hong Kong, we observe a variety of ways to define the regulatory scope of OTC derivatives regulation. Each jurisdiction has to identify ways to fit definitions of derivatives into existing regulatory systems. In Hong Kong, regulators built upon the existing legal framework to first define an OTC derivative product as a structured product, followed by a negative list of instruments that regulators did not wish to fall within the OTC derivatives regulations. On the whole, those definitions should catch most (if not all) derivatives in the market, although it may be unavoidable that some legal uncertainties could be waiting for market participants to explore in the future.

---

60   SFO Schedule 1 paragraph 1A (Hong Kong).
61   SFO Schedule 1 paragraph 1A (Hong Kong).
62   SFO Schedule 1 paragraph 1B(4) (Hong Kong).
63   SFO Schedule 1 paragraph 1B(2) (Hong Kong).

3 The Reporting Mandate

3.1 *General Introduction*

The purpose of the reporting mandate is to improve the transparency of the derivatives market. Amid the many factors contributing to the GFC, credit derivatives 'have been widely seen as the manifestations of financial innovation that were most heavily implicated in the amplification of the risks created by the collapse of the U.S. sub-prime mortgage market to other corners of the global financial system.'[64] The Federal Reserve Bank of New York noted that 'although OTC derivatives were not a central cause of the crisis, we find that weaknesses in the infrastructure of derivatives markets did exacerbate the crisis.'[65] In addition, it also noted that 'the complexity and limited transparency of the market reinforced the potential for excessive risk-taking, as regulators did not have a clear view into how OTC derivatives were being traded.'[66] The regulators might have obtained some aggregate data published by the ISDA or by the BIS, but they did not have data on trading activities conducted by major market participants or individual traders. They might have acquired some information from financial statements of some market participants.

Nonetheless, some market participants may not be required to publish a financial statement (e.g., some private equity funds). The reporting in a financial statement is also subject to accounting standards, and there is no uniform rule regarding the manner in which a company should present data. In addition, because making a trade requires at least two parties, financial statements could hardly inform regulators about individual trades and the functioning of the market in the micro-level. Regulators were thus left with a huge vacuum in their understanding and control of the OTC derivatives market. With the reporting mandate, traders must report their trades to a trade repository, from which regulators have access to trading information not only on an aggregate level but also for individual transactions.

Promoted by the G20 and the FSB, the reporting mandate has been implemented in major markets relatively faster than the clearing and trading mandates. In the U.S., the reporting mandate is prescribed by the DFA[67] followed by subsidiary regulations issued by the CFTC. In Europe, EMIR provides that

---

64 Avgouleas (n 6) 50.
65 Duffie D., Li A. and Lubke T., *Policy Perspectives on OTC Derivatives Market Infrastructure*, Federal Reserve Bank of New York Staff Reports No. 424 (March 2010) in https://www.newyorkfed.org/medialibrary/media/research/staff_reports/sr424.pdf.
66 *Id*.
67 DFA S 727, 7 USC 2(a)(13).

counterparties and central counterparties (CCPs) shall ensure that the details of any derivative contract that they have concluded (including any modification or termination) are reported to a trade repository no later than the working day after the conclusion (or modification or termination) of the contract.[68] The general rule was supplemented by technical standards issued by ESMA. In this section, we consider the reporting mandate in Singapore and Hong Kong. Instead of using a country-by-country analysis, we break down the rules into different major topics. Comparisons with U.S. or EU laws are made when indicated.

3.2 Legal Mandate and Jurisdiction Scope

In both Hong Kong and Singapore, the reporting mandate is structured under securities regulations. In Singapore, the SFA was amended in 2012 (effective from 31 October 2013) to provide a legal mandate of the reporting mandate.[69] Further regulation is published by the MAS in the Securities and Futures (Reporting of Derivatives Contracts) Regulations 2013 (SG Reporting Rules). A breach of the reporting obligation (by principal or agent as specified person) would lead to a fine not exceeding $50,000 with a further fine of no more than $5000 per day for continuing offences.[70] In Hong Kong, the SFO (Cap 571) was amended in 2014 to provide the legal foundation of the reporting mandate,[71] with the subsidiary regulations, the Securities and Futures (OTC Derivative Transactions—Reporting and Record Keeping Obligations) Rules (Cap 571AL) (HK Reporting Rules), issued by the Hong Kong Monetary Authority in 2015. If a prescribed person is found to have violated the reporting and record-keeping obligations, the regulator could apply to the Court of First Instance to impose a fine not exceeding HK$5 million.[72] In both markets, the law makes it clear that a breach of the reporting obligation would not make a contract void or voidable.[73]

Before we discuss the details of the regulations, we should first consider the jurisdictional scope of the reporting mandate in Hong Kong and Singapore. The jurisdiction scope defines how far a trade should be reportable in a market. In general, the jurisdiction scope should reflect the desire of the local regulator to regulate the local market. Therefore, it is natural that a trade will

---

68 EMIR art 9(1).
69 SFA s 125 *et seq* (Singapore).
70 SFA s 125(7) (Singapore).
71 SFO s 101B (Hong Kong).
72 SFO ss 101F and 101G (Hong Kong).
73 SFA s 125(10) (Singapore); SFO s 101B(7) (Hong Kong).

trigger the regulation of a particular country if it has an effect in that country. In other words, there must be some kind of local connection. However, different countries may have different ways to define a local connection.

In the U.S., under the DFA, the scope is defined by whether activities '... have a *direct and significant connection* with activities in, or effect on, commerce of the United States' (emphasis added).[74] Nonetheless, when making the subsidiary regulations, the CFTC focuses on the term 'U.S. person'. In other words, under the CFTC's current rule, if one of the parties to a trade is a U.S. person, the trade would be reportable under U.S. law. In contrast, in Europe, the jurisdiction scope of EU regulations regarding the reporting mandate is not clearly provided (unlike the clearing mandate[75]). If we interpret the terms 'counterparties' and 'CCPs' pursuant to its definition in the EMIR, it might mean that parties subject to the reporting mandate under EU law are counterparties and CCPs established in the EU.[76] If so, foreign parties are excluded from the reporting mandate under EU law.

Both Singapore and Hong Kong require certain connections with the local market to trigger the local reporting obligation. In Singapore, a derivative must be either traded in or booked in Singapore. Pursuant to SG Reporting Rules, 'traded in Singapore' means 'the execution of [a contract] by a trader whose place of employment is located in Singapore and who conducts... activities relating to the execution of derivatives contracts in Singapore' and who 'is physically in Singapore at the time of execution'.[77] In addition, 'booked in Singapore' means 'the entry of the derivatives contract on the balance sheet or the profit and loss accounts of a person whose place of business (including head office, branch, representative office or any kind of office[78]) is in Singapore.'[79] In short, the rule means that a trade should be reported pursuant to Singapore law if it is either physically conducted by a person in Singapore or is booked in Singapore accounts. Either way, it provides a connection with Singapore to trigger the obligation.

In Hong Kong, the jurisdiction base is defined in three ways. First, if a licensed corporation or authorised financial institution (see below[80]) is a

---

74 7 USC 2(i).
75 See EMIR art 4.
76 EMIR art 9 and art 2(1), (8) and (9).
77 Singapore Reporting Rules reg 2(1), amended by Securities and Futures (Reporting of Derivatives Contracts)(Amendment)(No 2) Regulations 2014.
78 Singapore Reporting Rules reg 2(1).
79 Singapore Reporting Rules reg 2(1).
80 See below Part III.C.2.

counterparty, such an institution is obliged to report the trade to the Hong Kong Monetary Authority (HKMA).[81] This is similar to the EU's position, in which the scope is marked by the nationality of a market participant. Second, a licensed corporation or authorised financial institution must disclose a trade if it is conducted 'on behalf of an affiliate of the [licensed corporation or authorised financial institution].'[82] In this case, the affiliate is a counterparty to the trade and 'one of the individuals who made the decision for the affiliate to enter into the transaction... acted in his or her capacity as a trader... and was employed or engaged by the person to perform his or her duties predominantly in Hong Kong.'[83] This rule also applies to situations in which a foreign financial institution trades a derivative on behalf of an affiliate.[84] Third, for a financial institution incorporated outside Hong Kong, the reporting obligation under Hong Kong law is applicable when the institution is a counterparty to a trade that is recorded in the books of its local branch or when the trade is conducted by an individual who made the trading decision in his capacity as a trader employed by an institution to perform his duties 'predominantly in Hong Kong.'[85] In the latter two cases, the rule is similar to that in Singapore, whereby a certain local connection is required.

In sum, the above discussion may show that Singapore and Hong Kong have adopted similar ways to define local connections to trigger the reporting mandate. This approach allow regulators in both markets to focus on transactions that would have some local impact of which regulators might need to know more information. This approach also suits both the markets' status as international financial and trading centres where people can move in and out easily. None of the countries chooses to provide an ultra-wide jurisdiction scope. This may be partly to avoid any deterrence effect and to avoid regulators from dealing with a lot of irrelevant information. In other words, this is a pragmatic choice.

3.3   Who—Reporting Parties

Who is obliged to report a trade that should be reported? There are a few paradigms to evaluate the meaning of 'reporting parties'. On the one hand, one question is whether non-financial institutions must report a derivative trade

---

81 Securities and Futures (OTC Derivative Transactions—Reporting and Record Keeping Obligations) Rules (Cap 571AL) rule 10(1) and 11(1). (HK Reporting Rules).
82 Id.
83 HK Reporting Rules rule 4(1).
84 HK Reporting Rules rule 12(1)(c).
85 HK Reporting Rules rule 12(1).

in addition to financial institutions. Whilst financial firms are clearly the main targets of the reporting mandate, non-financial firms may also trade considerable amounts of derivatives for hedging or other purposes. It is then left to policy-makers to decide whether to impose an obligation on a non-financial firm to report a trade. On the other hand, another threshold is whether a party (a financial or non-financial party) must trade a significant amount of derivatives to trigger the obligation. In other words, the policy question is whether to require reporting only from significant traders, while leaving out smaller players to save transaction costs. On this basis, we may compare the rules in Singapore and Hong Kong.

3.3.1   Singapore

In Singapore, a reporting party might be either the principal to a trade or his agent. The SFA requires a 'specified person' who is a party to a derivative contract to report a trade to a trade repository pursuant to regulations issued by the MAS.[86] By statutory definition, a 'specified person' includes licensed financial institutions under Singapore law, including banks, merchant banks, finance companies, insurance companies, approved trustees of collective investment schemes and holders of capital market licences.[87] Therefore, under Singapore law, those financial institutions are the main reporting parties.

In addition, a specified person includes 'any subsidiary of a bank incorporated in Singapore' and any other person designated by the MAS. The former covers all subsidiaries of a local bank, which may include both domestic and overseas subsidiaries. The rule seems to target the integrity of banks to avoid situations like Lehman Brothers, which set up specialist subsidiaries to trade derivatives, not only in the U.S. but also in the U.K. and Europe. However, Singapore law generally prohibits a bank from controlling non-financial firms,[88] so we expect banks' subsidiaries to be mostly financial businesses.

Regarding other non-financial parties, the MAS determines that a 'significant derivative holder' is also a 'specified person' under the SFA. By the regulator's definition, a 'significant derivative holder' is a resident of Singapore but is otherwise not a specified person, and his or her aggregate gross notional amount of trades booked or traded in Singapore has passed the reporting threshold in the previous quarter, which is set to be U.S.$8 billion (about U.S.$5.7 billion).[89] However, he would only cease to be a significant derivative holder if his trading

---

86 SFA s 125(1) (Singapore).
87 SFA s 124 (Singapore).
88 Banking Act s 30 (Singapore).
89 Singapore Reporting Rules reg 2 and 6(2).

OVER-THE-COUNTER DERIVATIVES REGULATION   19

volume failed to meet the reporting threshold for four consecutive quarters.[90] In other words, once a trader surpasses the reporting threshold, he or she becomes a 'significant derivative holder' (and thereby a 'specified person') from the next quarter. He or she would only lose this status by continuing to trade below the threshold in each quarter of a whole financial year.

If a 'specified person' is acting as an agent to a party of a trade, the agent also has a duty to report a trade if the principal party is not a specified person (or otherwise exempted), the specified person is incorporated in Singapore (or otherwise has a branch and office in Singapore) and the specified person enters into a trade through an individual employed or physically in Singapore.[91] The purpose of these conditions is to ensure that an agent only has the duty to report a trade when the party it represents has no obligation to report and the specified person (as an agent) has a local connection with Singapore (e.g., is incorporated or has a branch in Singapore).

There is a special exemption if a person (no matter as a principal or agent) is prohibited from reporting information by a specified jurisdiction before 1 July 2017.[92] The list of specified jurisdictions is shown in the Fifth Schedule of the Reporting Rules, including Algeria, Argentina, Austria, Bahrain, Belgium, France, Hungary, India, Luxembourg, Pakistan, the People's Republic of China, Samoa, Singapore, Switzerland and Taiwan.[93] Moreover, some governmental bodies or supra-national organisations are exempted from the reporting obligation, including governments or statutory boards, any central bank in the world, any central government, any public agency (for non-commercial purposes) established by a foreign government and a list of multilateral organisations (including the Asian Development Bank, the BIS, the European Investment Bank and the IMF).[94]

3.3.2 Hong Kong

In Hong Kong, the meaning of 'reporting parties' is similar to that in Singapore and is divided into two main groups: financial institutions and non-financial institutions. However, the rules regarding non-financial institutions have not yet come into effect at the time of writing.

First, the 2014 amendment of the SFO defines 'prescribed person' in relation to reporting obligations to include an authorised financial institution,

---

90   Singapore Reporting Rules reg 6(3).
91   SFA s 125(2) and (3) (Singapore).
92   Singapore Reporting Rule reg 11.
93   Singapore Reporting Rules Fifth Schedule.
94   Singapore Reporting Rules reg 10 and Fourth Schedule.

an approved money broker, a licensed corporation or a person of a class or description specified in the reporting rules.[95] Under the SFO, an 'authorised financial institution' (AI) means an authorised institution under s 2(1) of the Banking Ordinance (Cap 155),[96] which includes a bank, restricted license bank or a deposit-taking company.[97] Thus, the term 'authorised financial institution' captures banks and deposit-taking institutions. In addition, a 'licensed corporation' is defined in the SFO as 'a corporation which is granted a license under section 116 or 117 of [the SFO].'[98] This means a licensed corporation (which may include partnership or even sole proprietorship[99]) that holds capital market licences to carry on regulated activities under Hong Kong's securities regulations.[100] However, the definition of 'prescribed person' seems to leave out insurance companies, which are also not covered by the reporting rules issued by the HKMA, unless insurers are otherwise covered as a systemically important participant (see below). Pursuant to the reporting rules issued by the HKMA, a recognised clearing house or an ATS-CCP (i.e., one that provides automated trading and clearing services) is also obligated to report a trade.[101]

However, Hong Kong law also provides that a 'prescribed person' is regarded as an exempted person (to be exempted from trading a derivative as a counterparty[102]) if the sum of all of the notional amounts of all outstanding OTC derivative transactions within the prescribed product class (see next section) does not exceed U.S.$30 million and the person is not conducting trading on behalf of an affiliate.[103] In other words, Hong Kong law excludes financial institutions without a significant trading volume from the reporting obligation. This is not seen in Singapore.

Second, a party that is not otherwise a prescribed person may also be required to notify the regulator as a 'systemically important participant' if his or her trading positions pass a certain threshold.[104] However, in the 2015 version of the Reporting Rules, the HKMA did not include specific details about the application of this rule. Thus, as of mid-2016, the threshold for a systemically important participant remains unclear.

---

95   SFO s 101A (Hong Kong).
96   SFO Schedule 1 para 1 (Hong Kong).
97   Banking Ordinance (Cap 155) s 2(1) (Hong Kong).
98   SFO Schedule 1 (Hong Kong).
99   SFO Schedule 10 paragraphs 27–30 (Hong Kong).
100 See SFO ss 116 and 117 (Hong Kong).
101 HK Reporting Rules rule 5.
102 HK Reporting Rules rules 10(3) and 11(3).
103 HK Reporting Rules rule 3(2).
104 SFO ss 101A and 101R (Hong Kong).

3.3.3 Comparison

In sum, both Singapore and Hong Kong primarily target financial institutions as the main reporting parties. However, whilst Singapore's regulations cover may kinds of financial regulations, Hong Kong law seems to focus only on institutions covered by banking and securities regulations. The most critical result is that insurers in Singapore are in principle required to report a trade, whilst insurers in Hong Kong have no such requirement under the current regulations. In addition, unlike Hong Kong, Singapore offers no reporting threshold for financial institutions. Both Singapore and Hong Kong may require non-financial parties to report a trade. In Singapore, one is subject to the reporting obligation if he passes the reporting threshold. In Hong Kong, the rules are not yet finalised, but there is a legal mandate to allow the financial regulators to impose a similar requirement.

In sum, the infrastructure in Singapore is more comprehensive and akin to regulations in the U.S. and EU. For example, in the EU, the reporting obligation falls on counterparties and CCPs.[105] In the U.S., it is down to the parties and partly depends on the nature of a counterparty (e.g., being a swap dealer and/or a major swap participant) to determine the reporting party.[106] We may suggest that the reporting obligation for financial institutions may be in a way more limited in scope for financial institutions in Hong Kong.

3.4 What—Reportable Transactions

Once we identify the reporting parties, the next question is whether a trade is reportable. Although there is a general reporting mandate, it does not mean that each country requires the reporting of all kinds of derivatives transactions. For major markets in the U.K. and the U.S., there are clear incentives to require a wider range of products to be reported because those markets accommodate most of the world of derivatives trades of any kind. However, for smaller markets like Singapore and Hong Kong, it is debateable whether regulators need to prescribe the reporting of a wide range of transactions. After all, many products may have very little local relevance, so regulators may have no particular interest in those deals. In both markets, regulators have adopted a more incremental approach to the list of reportable trades.

Singapore adopted an incremental approach to the matter. In the original Reporting Rule, the reporting obligation applied only to interest rate and credit derivatives. In general, the choice of interest rate derivatives and credit derivatives meets the global trend; interest rate derivatives have the

---

105 EMIR art 9(1).
106 DFA s 727, 7 USC 2(a)(13)(F). See also 17 CFR 43.3(a)(3) (2012) and 17 CFR 45.8 (2012).

highest trading volume and credit derivatives were the culprit for the global financial crisis.

In 2014, the MAS expanded the scope to currency derivatives.[107] Because foreign exchange derivatives are popular in Asia amongst trade-oriented economies, the expansion made good sense. In 2016, the MAS further signalled its intention to expand the application of the reporting obligation to equity or commodity derivatives.[108] Therefore, through this incremental approach, the MAS started with interest rate and credit derivatives to cover most of the market before expanding into other reference variables to complete the regulatory structure. This allows regulators to refine regulatory rules and to absorb information and gives local and foreign market participants sufficient time to digest and adapt.

In contrast, Hong Kong's approach was much more restrictive, although still incremental in nature. In the 2015 Reporting Rules, the HKMA intended only to apply the reporting obligation to interest rate swaps and non-deliverable forwards (NDFS).[109] According to Hong Kong Monetary Authority's first consultation paper in 2011, foreign exchange derivatives amount to 58% of trading (by notional value) in Hong Kong, followed by interest rate swaps (18%) and NDFS (17%).[110] However, since foreign exchange derivatives (other than NDFS) tended to be 'very short-dated and settled through the Continuous Linked settlement system..., they are considered to be less of a concern.'[111] As a result, Hong Kong focuses the next largest classes of OTC derivatives, i.e. interest rate swaps and NDFS.[112] However, this also means that the scope of Hong Kong's reporting obligation is much more limited than not only major Western markets but also Singapore, its main Asian competitor.

In September 2015, Hong Kong's regulators declared their intention to expand the reporting mandate (i.e., phase 2 reporting) to capture major asset classes including interest rates, foreign exchange, equity, credit and commodity

---

107 Singapore Reporting Rules reg 5. Foreign exchange derivatives was included in November 2014 pursuant to Securities and Futures (Reporting of Derivatives Contracts) (Amendment)(No 2) Regulations 2014.
108 Monetary Authority of Singapore, 'Proposed Amendments to the Securities & Futures (Reporting of Derivatives Contracts) Regulations (P002–2016)' (2016), http://www.mas.gov.sg/News-and-Publications/Consultation-Paper/2016/Consultation-Paper-on-Proposed-Amendments-to-the-SF-Reporting-of-Derivatives-Contracts-Regulations.aspx.
109 HK Reporting Rules Schedule 1.
110 Above n 34, at 14.
111 Id.
112 Id.

derivatives.[113] When fully implemented, it will eliminate any remaining differences between the scope of the reporting mandates in Hong Kong and those of other major markets, including Singapore.

3.5 *Compliance Issues*

Once we identify the reporting parties and reportable trades, some compliance issues remain, including when to report, how to report, what to report and to whom to report. In this section, we analyse those issues separately. In particular, we also consider the issues of back-loading and substituted compliance. The latter is a particular issue that faces smaller derivatives markets like Singapore and Hong Kong.

3.5.1 Timing and Back-loading

There are some issues regarding the timing of reporting. First, regarding the deadline to report a trade if it is reportable, regulators would naturally prefer parties to report a trade as soon as they can. In Singapore, a party is expected to report a trade within two business days after the execution or termination of a trade.[114] In Hong Kong, the rule requires a party to report a trade on a T+2 basis.[115] In this regard, both markets are on the same page.

Second, there are issues about outstanding transactions conducted before the effective day of the reporting obligation. This relates to the issue of 'back-loading', which has some practical importance for banks in determining the scope of past proprietary or client transactions that should be reported upon the implementation of the reporting rules. In Hong Kong, the regulator takes a very simple approach that all outstanding trades on the starting day of the Reporting Rules should be reported.[116] To smooth out the formal implementation, the HKMA also designed a concession period for first-time reporting parties.[117]

In contrast, in Singapore, reportable derivatives entered into before the day of enforcement of the mandate but with more than 1 year of maturity

---

113 Hong Kong Securities and Futures Commission, 'Consultation Conclusions and Further Consultation on Introducing Mandatory Clearing and Expanding Mandatory Reporting' (2016), at [130], http://www.sfc.hk/edistributionWeb/gateway/EN/consultation/doc?refNo=16CP1.
114 Singapore Reporting Rules reg 9 and Third Schedule.
115 HK Reporting Rules rule 25(1).
116 HK Reporting Rules rules 10(2), 11(2), 12(2).
117 HK Reporting Rules rules 22–25.

remaining at the reporting commencement date must be reported.[118] Upon the implementation of relevant rules, a party is given six months to report those outstanding trades after the reporting commencement date.[119] Thus, in effect, the back-loading rules in Singapore and Hong Kong are generally similar to cover outstanding trades with more than 1 year of maturity.

Regardless of the differences, the back-loading rules are most important close to the implementation date of the reporting rules or the date when the rules are expanded to cover other products. Their importance diminishes over time because most past transactions will have matured.

3.5.2 How to Report: Single-sided or Dual Reporting

Another important compliance issue is whether both parties are required to report or whether it is sufficient for one party to report the trade. The former is 'single-sided reporting', whilst the latter is the two-sided reporting approach. Single-sided reporting has the benefits of simplicity and lower transaction costs, because only one party is required to make the report. However, data accuracy may be challenged at times because the trade repository only has information from one side. The reverse is true for the two-sided reporting approach. Whilst transaction costs may be higher and a trade repository must handle duplicate reports of trades, trading information may be more precise because there are at least two reports of the same trade.

In Singapore, a trade is deemed to have been reported if a specified person (A) has reported that information to another person (B) and B has reported that information to a trade repository, as long as the information reported is true and correct.[120] Moreover, a person is deemed to have complied with the reporting obligation if any other person who is obliged by the reporting obligation has reported the trade truthfully.[121] In this situation, the reporting obligation is deemed to have been complied with when the information is received by a trade repository.[122] Therefore, Singapore clearly adopts the single-sided reporting approach. The rules in this paragraph also open the room for a transaction party or agents to have separate agreements to arrange the reporting of a trade.

In contrast, in Hong Kong, the reporting obligation is imposed upon the 'prescribed person'. If a party is a prescribed person, he or she must report a

---

118 Singapore Reporting Rules Third Schedule.
119 Id.
120 SFA s 125(4) (Singapore).
121 SFA s 125(5) (Singapore).
122 SFA s 125(6) (Singapore).

trade regardless of whether the other party is a prescribed person.[123] This also means that both parties must report a reportable trade if both of them are prescribed persons. Whilst Hong Kong's regulators seem to prefer data accuracy to convenience, it remains to be seen whether this will cause any chance of arbitrage, at least between Hong Kong and Singapore.

3.5.3   Information to be Reported

In Singapore, information that should be reported includes contract information, counterparties, clearing status and transactional data.[124] In Hong Kong, the Reporting Rules require transaction information such as the dates of the transactions and maturity, the trading platform and identifying references, clearing status, subsequent events, transactional terms (e.g., notional amount or currency) and the parties.[125]

To unify the manner in which data are reported and to increase the comparability of data, some efforts have been made to standardise the information to be reported. To this end, the FSB has been working on a standard format of reporting, including a universal system of legal entity identifiers for firms around the world. To create such a system, the FSB has set up the Legal Entity Identifier Regulatory Oversight Committee.[126] The ISDA is also working on standard forms and standards to facilitate the clearing and reporting of OTC derivatives.[127] Hong Kong and Singapore will probably adopt the standards used by other global trade repositories (the Singapore repository is actually operated by DTCC, a U.S. trade repository operator), as both countries accept the use of the 'unique transaction identifier' (UTI) for reporting purposes.

---

123   Hong Kong Monetary Authority, *Frequently Asked Questions on the Securities and Future* (OTC *Derivative Transactions—Reporting and Record Keeping Obligations*) *Rules*, at Q14 (10 Jul 2015), http://www.hkma.gov.hk/media/eng/doc/key-information/guidelines-and-circular/2015/20150710e1.pdf.
124   Singapore Reporting Rules First Schedule.
125   HK Reporting Rules Schedule 1 Part 4.
126   The Legal Entity Identifier Regulatory Oversight Committee—LEI ROC, http://www.leiroc.org/.
127   For example, the ISDA has published the Clearing Connectivity Standard to help facilitate the clearing and reporting of OTC derivatives. *See* the ISDA website, https://www2.isda.org/functional-areas/technology-infrastructure/clearing-connectivity-standard-ccs/. *See also* ISDA Cleared Swap Documentation, http://www.isda.org/publications/isda-cleared-swap.aspx.

3.5.4 Report to Whom and Substituted Compliance

In general, information about trading should be reported to a trade repository. Nonetheless, a bigger question is whether it is required to report to the local trade repository or whether it is sufficient if a reporting party reports a trade to a foreign trade repository. The latter raises the issue of 'substituted compliance' (i.e., complying with local regulations by submitting information to a foreign trade repository).

Substituted compliance is a particular problem for smaller markets like Hong Kong and Singapore. Because banks in the U.S., U.K., and Europe dominate the market as major derivatives dealers, local traders in Asia are most likely to be trading with Western counterparties. However, those Western counterparties are obliged by American and European regulations to report their trades to a trade repository in the U.S. or Europe. It is natural that those Western counterparties might prefer to report a trade in the U.S. or Europe to comply with their regulations. As a result, an Asian trader may have no choice but to accept reporting the trade to a Western trade repository. This may have the effect of maintaining the dominance of major markets.[128]

This leaves Asian regulators with a dilemma. On the one hand, requiring local traders and Western counterparties to report a trade to a local trade repository in Asia might simply force Western counterparties to withdraw from the market, if reporting to an Asian trade repository cannot substitute for the compliance with the reporting obligation in the U.S. or the EU. On the other hand, Asian regulators may be forced to accept substituted compliance if they aim to compete for a larger market share, even though substituted compliance might mean that less information is immediately available for the regulator's perusal.

Therefore, the issue of substituted compliance will rise to the fore. In general, the recognition of substituted compliance is built upon equivalence and mutual recognition. In Singapore, substituted compliance is allowed under certain conditions. The SFA provides that a specified person shall be deemed to have complied with the reporting obligation if any other party (or the principal party, if the specified person is an agent) is incorporated under a foreign law and any party to the transaction is required to comply with the law of that foreign country to report a trade.[129] In short, Singapore allows for substituted compliance if the other party to a trade is a foreign person who is obliged to

---

[128] Nichols C., 'Mutual Recognition Based on Substituted Compliance: An Integral Component of the SEC's Mandate' (2008) 34 *North Carolina Journal of International Law & Commercial Regulation* 1 1, 7.

[129] SFA s 128(1) and (2) (Singapore).

report a trade pursuant to the laws in his home country. In contrast, in Hong Kong, the HKMA is determined from the beginning to prescribe for local reporting to the trade repository set up under the HKMA.[130]

The differences between the two markets certainly reflects the regulatory dilemma described above. The reason why Singapore opts to accept substituted compliance might be partly the market reality and partly the desire to compete for more derivatives to further raise Singapore's profile as a financial centre and trading hub. In contrast, Hong Kong's regulator focuses on acquiring first-hand information.[131] The MAS attempts to resolve the potential lack of information by cross-regulatory cooperation. For example, the MAS signed a memorandum of understanding with the Australia Securities and Investments Commission in 2014 to this effect.[132] Whether the differences will alter the development of the market in Asia and whether it would enhance or reduce systemic risk[133] remain to be seen, although it is an interesting development to monitor in the future.

4 Clearing Mandate

4.1 *General Introduction*

The purpose of the clearing mandate is to address counterparty risk OTC derivatives. Without a clearing house, the parties to an OTC trade must underwrite the other party's credit risk, which can be quite significant as the trading volume grows. Under the ISDA form, the fundamental method of controlling credit risk is the application of payment netting and the option of early termination of all trades by the non-defaulting party.[134] Payment netting might reduce a party's overall exposure to credit risk to the net amount owed to or by either party. Early termination allows a party to quit all trades under one contract when something goes wrong to limit the damage (although the

---

[130] HK Reporting Rules rule 20.
[131] Hong Kong Securities and Futures Commission, 'Consultation Conclusions and Further Consultation on the Securities and Futures (OTC Derivative Transactions—Reporting and Record Keeping Obligations) Rules' at 59, http://www.sfc.hk/edistributionWeb/gateway/EN/consultation/doc?refNo=14CP8.
[132] See MAS announcement on September 17, 2014, at http://www.mas.gov.sg/News-and-Publications/Media-Releases/2014/ASIC-and-mas-sign-World-First-Memorandum-of-Understanding.aspx.
[133] See generally Griffith S. J., 'Substituted Compliance and Systemic Risk: How to Make a Global Market in Derivative Regulation' (2014) 98 *Minnesota Law Review* 1291.
[134] ISDA Master Agreement (2002 Edition) ss 2(c), 5 and 6.

non-defaulting party may still suffer some losses when they close out all outstanding trades). The regime generally seems to work well, as there has been little litigation regarding the widely popular ISDA master agreement over the past three decades. However, the global financial crisis exposed shortcomings. For example, in the case of the resolution of Lehman Brothers, it was estimated that the net worth of Lehman Brothers' OTC derivatives positions at the time of bankruptcy was about U.S.$ 20.3 billion, and even after two years there remained more than 1,000 contracts not finally settled.[135] To prevent losses from spreading too soon and to curtail systemic risk, the solution is to push OTC trades into the clearing system. This idea seems to be drawn from the futures market, in which futures exchanges provide a forum for trade before pushing all trades to be cleared by a clearing house or CCP. Typically, in the futures market, once a contract is made between two traders, the contract is then novated into two contracts. The novation process continues until the point at which the CCP becomes the ultimate counterparty to all contracts. To control credit risk, a margin requirement is commonly required by a CCP (or central security depository, exchanges or matching platforms) on a clearing member to pay a certain sum of money or liquid assets into a margin account. The value of the margin account is marked to the market on a daily basis to reflect profits or losses incurred by the trader. If the amount in the margin account drops below a certain level, it might trigger a margin call that requests the member to post more collateral. Otherwise the CCP may close out of his or her trading positions to stop further losses. This is an essential feature of the futures market to ensure the solvency and soundness of the futures market and the clearing system. In other words, with the margin requirement, a CCP seeks to curtail losses from credit risk at an earlier stage.

It is understandable that the clearing system appeals to policymakers when designing a new regulatory structure for OTC derivatives. On the one hand, it is rare to find a CCP collapsing. Only three incidents have been reported in the past century (the latest in 1989).[136] On the other hand, futures exchanges, the market for exchange-traded derivatives, seem to work very well, with higher transparency and fewer legal troubles throughout the years. Therefore, centralised clearing looks like a safe option. However, a CCP is certainly not always bulletproof; there could be human errors. If a bank like Lehman Brothers

---

135 Fleming M. J. and Sarkar A., *The Failure Resolution of Lehman Brothers*, FRBNY Economic Policy Review (Dec 2014), 175, 184, in https://www.newyorkfed.org/medialibrary/media/research/staff_reports/sr424.pdf.

136 Wendt F., 'Central Counterparties: Addressing Their Too Important to Fail Nature' (2015) WP/15/21, at 11(note 7), https://www.imf.org/external/pubs/ft/wp/2015/wp1521.pdf.

is already 'too big to fail', a giant CCP may be an even larger mammoth to fail if we pool most OTC trades into the clearing system.[137] Some have cautioned that CCPs are not panaceas and they have their own vulnerabilities.[138] Professor Roe describes it as 'clearinghouse overconfidence'.[139] Even worse, leading market CCPs may clear trades from all corners of the world, which makes the regulation of large CCPs not only a domestic regulatory issue but also an international one. There could also be considerable issues of clearing non-standardised bespoke OTC derivatives.[140] Some went further to suggest a more decentralised risk management approach.[141] Whether CCPs may or should have access to central bank liquidity remains an issue.[142] Those factors may affect the implementation of the clearing mandate in smaller markets. Braithwaite also suggests that 'concluding from all this momentum that the CCP prescription is one of the more uncontroversial or straightforward elements of the public sector's legislative response to the financial crisis would be a mistake.'[143]

On this basis, we introduce current regulations on the clearing mandate in Singapore and Hong Kong. We should be aware that regulators in both markets have not fully implemented the clearing mandate. In Singapore, draft rules were published in a consultation paper in July 2015. Hong Kong did a similar

---

137 See generally Wendt, *id.*; Chamorro-Courtland C., 'The Trillion Dollar Question: Can A Central Bank Bail Out A Central Counterparty Clearing House Which Is "Too Big to Fail"?' (2012) 6 Brooklyn Journal of Corporate, Financial & Commercial Law 433; Yadav Y., 'The Problematic Case of Clearinghouses in Complex Markets' (2013) 101 Georgetown Law Journal 387; Nichol A., 'Hedging against the Next Financial Crisis: Proposals for Managing Systemic Risk in Centrally Cleared Derivatives Transactions' (2013) 29 *Banking and Finance Law Review* 169.

138 Pirrong C., 'The Economics of Central Clearing: Theory and Practice', at 11, http://www2.isda.org/news/isda-publishes-the-economics-of-central-clearing-theory-and-practice-a-discussion-paper-on-clearing-issues.

139 Roe M. J., 'Clearinghouse Overconfidence' (2013) 101 *California Law Review* 1641.

140 Le Vine B., 'The Derivative Market's Black Sheep: Regulation of Non-Cleared Security-Based Swap under Dodd-Frank' (2011) 31 *Northwestern Journal of International Law and Business* 699, 716–717.

141 See e.g. Manns J., 'Insuring against a Derivative Disaster: The Case for Decentralised Risk Management' (2013) 98 *Iowa Law Review* 1575.

142 See e.g. Kress J. C., 'Credit Default Swaps, Clearinghouses, and Systemic Risk: What Centralised Counterparties Must Have Access to Central Bank Liquidity?' (2011) 48 *Harvard Journal on Legislation* 49.

143 Braithwaite J. P., 'The Inherent Limits of "Legal Devices": Lessons for the Public Sector's Central Counterparty Prescription for the OTC Derivatives Markets' (2011) 12 *European Business Organisation Law Review* 87, 90–91.

thing in September 2015. However, in both markets the rules are not finalised as of June 2016. Thus, we have only limited means to make a detailed comparison. In the sections below, we introduce basic regulations regarding the clearing mandate in both markets based on existing legislation and draft clearing rules. For issues that overlap with the reporting mandate, we only introduce the differences to avoid duplication.

4.2   Legal Mandate and Jurisdiction Scope

A clear legal mandate to implement the clearing obligation requires parties to submit an otherwise bilateral trade to a CCP. In the U.S., the mandate is provided in the DFA,[144] whilst in Europe, it is stated in the EMIR.[145] In Singapore, the SFA provides that '[e]very specified person who is a party to a specified derivatives contract shall... cause the specified derivatives contract to undergo clearing by... an approved clearing house...'[146] In Hong Kong, s 101C of the SFO provides that a 'prescribed person' must clear an OTC derivative transaction that is specified by the clearing rules issued by regulators with a designated CCP in accordance with the clearing rules.[147] However, several years after the amendment of the law, the clearing mandate has not yet been fully implemented in Singapore. In Hong Kong, the regulators only implemented subsidiary regulations in September 2016.[148] At the end of this section, we explore some probable reasons.

As with the reporting mandate, there is a question on the jurisdiction scope of the clearing obligation, especially when a trade is conducted in a foreign market. As mentioned earlier, the scope of the DFA is defined by the meaning of 'U.S. person'.[149] In Europe, the EMIR provides that a contract must be cleared by a CCP if it is concluded between two European parties who are financial counterparties or non-financial counterparties that meet the clearing threshold.[150] If one party is not a European entity (and the other is an eligible European entity), a trade must still be cleared if the foreign party 'would be subject to the clearing obligation if it were established in the [EU].'[151] When both

---

144   DFA s 723(h)(1), 12 USC 2(h)(1).
145   EMIR Recital 13 and art 4.
146   SFA s 129C(1).
147   Securities and Futures Ordinance s 101C(1) and (2) (Hong Kong).
148   Securities and Futures (OTC Derivative Transactions—clearing and Record Keeping Obligations and Designation of Central Counterparties) Rules (Cap 571AN). (HK Clearing Rules).
149   See above Part III.B.
150   EMIR art 4(1)(a)(i) to (iii).
151   EMIR art 4(1)(a)(iv).

parties are from outside the EU, a trade must be cleared pursuant to European regulations if both parties would be subject to the clearing obligation if they were established in the EU, provided that the contract has a 'direct, substantial and foreseeable effect' in the EU or when it is necessary and appropriate.[152]

What amounts to such a 'direct, substantial and foreseeable effect'? A further delegated regulation provides some solutions.[153] First, if an entity (X) in a third country is guaranteed by entities (Y) established within the EU, a contract entered into by X would be considered to have a substantial effect in the EU when the amount of guarantee surpasses a certain threshold, because this amounts to financial risks that face Y.[154] Against this context, a guarantee is defined as 'an explicit documented legal obligation by a guarantor to cover payments ... due or that may become due pursuant to the OTC derivative contracts covered by that guarantee and entered into by the guaranteed entity ... .'[155] An OTC transaction is considered to have a direct, substantial and foreseeable effect within the EU when at least one third-country entity benefits from the guarantee (wholly or partially) provided by a financial counterparty established in the EU if the following two conditions are met: (a) the guarantee covers at least Euro 8 million of aggregated notional amount; and (b) the guarantee is at least equal to 5% of the sum of the current exposure (defined in art 272(17) of Regulation 575/2013) in the OTC derivative contracts of the financial counterparty (guarantor) established in the EU.[156]

Because only Hong Kong has published final rules on clearing obligation as of December 2016, we cannot comment on the manner in which both markets will define the regulatory scope. In Singapore, the draft regulations published in July 2015, a contract might have to be cleared pursuant to Singapore law if it is 'booked in Singapore', which is defined as 'the entry of the derivatives contract on the balance sheet or the profit and loss accounts of a person ... who is a party to the derivatives contract; and whose place of business ... is in Singapore.'[157] If this becomes the final rule, the jurisdiction scope would be more limited than that of the reporting obligation under Singapore law. This

---

152 EMIR art 4(1)(a)(v).
153 Commission Delegated Regulation (EU) No 285/2014.
154 Commission Delegated Regulation (EU) No 285/2014 recital 5.
155 Commission Delegated Regulation (EU) No 285/2014 art 1.
156 Commission Delegated Regulation (EU) No 285/2014 art 2.
157 Reg 2 and First Schedule of Draft Securities and Futures (Clearing of Derivatives Contracts) Regulations 2015, in Annex B to Monetary Authority of Singapore, 'Draft Regulations for Mandatory Clearing of Derivatives Contracts (P010–2015)', http://www.mas.gov.sg/News-and-Publications/Consultation-Paper/2015/Consultation-Paper-on-Draft-Regulations-for-Mandatory-Clearing-of-Derivatives-Contracts.aspx. (Singapore Draft Clearing Rules).

also shows that the MAS only requires the clearing of specified OTC derivatives if it has some financial effect on Singaporean entities (because the trade is booked in Singapore).

In Hong Kong, the clearing rules published in 2016 provide that a trade should be cleared if a party is a 'prescribed person' (see next section) or when 'the transaction is recorded in the form of an entry in the Hong Kong books of the person' if the person is an overseas financial institution.[158] In other words, a trade should be cleared under Hong Kong law if it is conducted by a financial institution in Hong Kong or if it is booked in Hong Kong. Either way provides a connection with the Hong Kong market. The positions in Singapore and Hong Kong are similar in this regard.

4.3 Who—Clearing Parties and Clearing Threshold

As with the reporting obligation, we must first define the parties who would be obliged to submit a trade for clearing. In the U.S., the CFTC divides the clearing parties into two categories. Category 1 entities include swap dealers (including security-based swap dealers), major swap participants (including major security-based swap participants) and active funds,[159] and category 2 entities include commodity pools, private funds (defined in s 202(a) of the Investment Advisers Act) and persons who engage predominantly in banking activities.[160] An active fund is any private fund defined in s 202(a) of the Investment Advisers Act of 1940 that is not a third-party subaccount[161] (i.e., for the fund's own account) and that executes 200 or more swaps per month based on a monthly average over the past 12 months.[162] Thus, the U.S. requires mostly financial institutions and funds that engage in significant derivatives trading to submit trades to clearing.

In Europe, the EMIR provides that '[c]ounterparties shall clear all OTC derivative contracts ...' if these contracts satisfy certain conditions.[163] The clearing obligation may apply to both a 'financial counterparty' or a 'non-financial counterparty' (where appropriate).[164] Unless otherwise exempted (see below),

---

158   HK Clearing Rules rule 6(1)(a).
159   17 CFR 50.25(a) (2012).
160   17 CFR 50.25(a) (2012).
161   A 'third party subaccount' means an account that is managed by an investment manager that is independent and unaffiliated with the account's beneficiary or sponsor. 17 CFR 50.25 (2012).
162   17 CFR 50.25(a) (2012).
163   EMIR article 4.
164   EMIR recital 29.

the clearing obligation applies if a contract is between two 'financial counterparties'.[165] The term 'financial counterparty' generally indicates financial institutions, including investment firms, credit institutions (i.e., banks), insurance or assurance undertakings (i.e., insurance companies and reinsurers), collective investment schemes, occupational retirement pension operators and alternative investment funds.[166]

If one or both parties is a non-financial counterparty[167], the non-financial counterparty must pass a prescribed clearing threshold,[168] which is set to reflect the systemic relevance of the sum of net positions and the exposure of a firm.[169] Once a non-financial counterparty passes the clearing threshold, the firm should immediately notify the ESMA and a local regulator, and the firm will be subject to the clearing obligation.[170] Clearing should begin 4 months after qualification for the clearing obligation.[171] A non-financial counterparty is no longer subject to the clearing obligation if the firm's rolling average position over 30 working days does not exceed the clearing threshold.[172] For calculation purposes, the firm should include all OTC derivative contracts and exposure of the other non-financial counterparty in the same group to have a fair measure of total risk exposure.[173] Further details are provided in the technical standards published by the ESMA.[174]

In Singapore, a 'specified person' is subject to the clearing obligation. However, there is a slight difference between the definition of 'specified person' for the reporting and clearing obligations[175]. Unlike the reporting obligation, 'any subsidiary of a bank incorporated in Singapore' (which is a specified person under the reporting obligation) is not a 'specified person' under the clearing obligation. However, the statutory list of 'specified persons' covers mainly financial institutions, from banks and insurers to approved trustees and holders of capital market licences.[176] Even though the MAS has the power

---

165 The term is defined in EMIR article 2(8).
166 EMIR art 2(8).
167 Defined in EMIR article 2(9).
168 EMIR article 4(1)(a), referring to article 10(1)(b).
169 EMIR recital 31.
170 EMIR art 10(1).
171 EMIR art 10(1)(c).
172 EMIR art 10(2).
173 EMIR art 10(3).
174 EMIR art 10(4).
175 *Cf.* SFA ss 124 and 129B (Singapore).
176 SFA s 124 (Singapore).

to prescribe other non-financial institutions to be a 'specified person',[177] it has not yet exercised that power in the draft regulations published in July 2015.

However, the MAS proposes to exempt specified persons (even if they are financial institutions) with fewer trades from the clearing obligation if the person fails to meet the clearing threshold for four consecutive quarters.[178] The clearing threshold was proposed to be U.S.$20 billion.[179] In addition, governments or public bodies, central banks in other countries and some supranational organisations will also be exempt from the clearing obligation.[180] For clarification, the MAS exempts a trade from clearing if either party is an exempted person.[181]

In Hong Kong, in relation to the clearing obligation, a 'prescribed person' is an authorised financial institution, an approved money broker, a licensed corporation or a person or class prescribed by the regulator.[182] The meaning to some of those terms has been discussed in the section on reporting obligations.

In the new clearing rules, Hong Kong's regulator only requires a trade to be cleared if it is between a prescribed person and another prescribed person or a 'financial services provider'.[183] 'Financial services providers' are subject to the regulator's designation. For simplicity and clarity, the HKSFC publishes a list of these financial services providers in the consultation. The list mainly includes global banks and their subsidiary operations.[184]

Similar to Singapore, Hong Kong also plans to have a clearing threshold, proposed to be U.S.$20 billion over the past 6 months.[185] When counting the threshold, the HKSFC proposes that the entire portfolio will be counted rather than calculating only one type of derivative.[186] An eligible firm may give an exit notice if it trades less than U.S.$14 billion for consecutive 12 months.[187] It also does not matter whether a trade is conducted in or outside Hong Kong.[188]

---

177 SFA s 129 (Singapore).
178 Singapore Draft Clearing Rules Second Schedule para 7.
179 Singapore Draft Clearing Rules reg 2.
180 Singapore Draft Clearing Rules Second Schedule para 1 to 6.
181 Singapore Draft Clearing Rules reg 7.
182 SFO s 101A (Hong Kong).
183 HK Clearing Rules rule 6(1).
184 HKSFC (n 113) Appendix D.
185 HK Clearing Rules Schedule 2; HKSFC (n 113) [91].
186 HKSFC (n 113) [82].
187 HK Clearing Rules rule 6(3).
188 HK Clearing Rules rule 7.

4.4 Transactions Subject to the Clearing Obligation and Exempted Transactions

In this section, we consider transactions that are subject to the clearing obligation and certain exempted transactions. Apart from the clearing threshold and some exempted persons (discussed in the previous section), we consider whether Singapore and/or Hong Kong adopt the end-user exemption or the intragroup exemption seen in the EU and the U.S.

4.4.1 General

We will not repeat certain definitional issues discussed in previous sections. In short, not all OTCs are subject to the clearing obligation, even in the U.S. and Europe. One main reason is that there must be sufficient trades to offset opposing positions to make centralised clearing work and to ensure the safety of the clearing system. In the U.S., the classes of swaps that are subject to the clearing obligation as of June 2016 include mainly certain types of interest rate derivatives and credit default swaps with certain specifications (e.g., North American untranched CDS indices).[189] In Europe, the ESMA publishes the list in a public register. As of 11 May 2016 (the latest list at the time of writing), products that have been authorised for clearance by CCPs in Europe include some forms of interest rate derivatives and credit default swaps.[190]

In Singapore, the draft regulations published in July 2015 only indicated interest rate derivatives that either refer to the Singapore Swap Offered Rate (SOR) in Singapore dollars or the London Interbank Offered Rate (LIBOR) traded in U.S. dollars.[191] Nonetheless, the proposed regulations do not yet include credit default swaps. Although we do not have details of the market data, the decision may be partly because Singapore does not have a large market of credit default swaps and partly because interest rate derivatives are the most traded derivatives in Singapore.

At the initial stage, the HKSFC only focuses on some forms of interest rate derivatives to be subject to the clearing obligation.[192] Non-deliverable forwards, though reportable, are not subject to the clearing obligation in phase 1.[193] In this regard, Hong Kong and Singapore adopt a similar approach, at least in the

---

189   17 CFR 50.4 (2012).
190   See ESMA website: https://www.esma.europa.eu/sites/default/files/library/public_register_for_the_clearing_obligation_under_emir.pdf.
191   Singapore Draft Clearing Rules First Schedule.
192   HK Clearing Rules rule 4 and Schedule 1; HKSFC (n 113) [53].
193   HKSFC (n 113) [69].

initial stage. Whether both markets will expand the scope of clearable trades, as in the case of the reporting mandate, remains unclear.

4.4.2 Hedging or End-user Exemption

Some countries have an end-user exemption to exclude hedging transactions from the clearing obligation. This can be partly explained on the basis that a derivative transaction in theory should not hurt a firm's financial condition if it is a true hedging transaction, meaning that the trade would be used to offset losses that may arise from another source. In other words, if a trade is not purely speculative, some regulators will allow the deal to stay out of the clearing system to avoid disrupting hedging activities that might potentially beneficial to society.

In the U.S., a party may trigger the end-user exemption if it uses a derivative to hedge or to mitigate commercial risk, provided that the party is not a financial entity[194] and the trade is reported to a trade repository.[195] This is the so-called end-user exception.[196] To determine whether a transaction is used to hedge or mitigate commercial risk, a trade must be 'economically appropriate to the reduction of risks in the conduct and management of a commercial enterprise where the risk arises...', if the trade qualifies as *bona fide* hedging for purposes of an exemption from the position limit or if it is deemed as hedging under the GAAP accounting rules.[197]

In Europe, there seems to be no clear end-user exception as in the U.S. However, a non-financial counterparty may exclude true hedging positions from the calculation of the clearing threshold.[198] Therefore, the implication is that a non-financial firm's hedging activities would not trigger the clearing obligation because they are not counted toward the clearing threshold. For this purpose, 'consideration should be given to whether an OTC derivative contract is economically appropriate for the reduction of risks in the conduct and management of a non-financial counterparty, where the risks relate to fluctuations in interest rates, foreign exchange rates, inflation rates or commodity prices.'[199]

Both Singapore and Hong Kong have not proposed an end-user exemption.[200] In this regard, neither market has taken the same approach as the U.S., nor

---

194   DFA s 723(a)(3), 7 USC 2(h)(7)(C)(i).
195   17 CFR 50.50 and 39.6.
196   DFA s 723(3), 7 USC 2(h)(7)(A).
197   17 CFR 50.50(c)(1).
198   EMIR art 10(3).
199   EMIR recital 30.
200   See Singapore Draft Clearing Rules reg 7.

does it seem to be akin to the EU's approach by deducting hedging transactions from the calculation of the clearing threshold. Hong Kong's regulator makes it clear that '[t]he purpose of the threshold calculation is to help identify who are the most active dealers in the OTC derivatives market' and that '[t]his cannot be achieved if such transactions are disregarded.'[201] This statement underlines the standpoint in Hong Kong and Singapore.

4.4.3 Intragroup or Affiliate Exemptions

Another common exemption is to exclude derivatives transactions within the same group from the clearing obligation. In the U.S., this is called the 'affiliate exemption'. In Europe, it is called the 'intra-group exemption'. The purpose of this exemption seems to offer more flexibility to a firm's risk management strategies to improve efficiency. As the EU points out, it may be necessary 'for aggregating risks within a group structure and that intragroup risks are therefore specific', as long as it does not raise systemic risk.[202]

In Europe, the EMIR provides that 'OTC derivative contracts that are intragroup transactions... shall not be subject to the clearing obligation.'[203] This exemption applies when the two parties belong to the same group and when they have notified or have been authorised by a competent regulator at least 30 days in advance.[204] A regulator has the power to object.[205] An intragroup transaction is also exempted from the requirements about risk mitigation and collateral even if a trade is not subject to the clearing obligation, provided that it does not increase systemic risk and provided that there is no current or foreseen practical or legal impediment to the prompt transfer of funds between the parties.

The EMIR offers two definitions for 'intragroup transactions', one for non-financial counterparties and one for financial counterparties. For a non-financial counterparty, an intragroup[206] transaction is an OTC derivative contract entered into with another counterparty that is part of the same group, provided that both parties are included in the same consolidation on a full basis

---

201 HKSFC (n 113) at [14].
202 EMIR recital 38.
203 EMIR art 4(2).
204 EMIR art 4(2). See also Delegated Regulation 149/2013 art 18 to 20.
205 EMIR art 4(2)(a). See also Commission Delegated Regulation (EU) No 149/2013 art 18 to 19.
206 A 'group' is defined by the EMIR as the group of undertakings consisting of a parent undertaking and its subsidiaries within the meaning of Articles 1 and 2 of the Seventh Directive on Consolidated Accounts) (83/349/EEC). EMIR art 2(16). See EMIR art 2(21) and (22) for further definition on 'parent undertaking' and 'subsidiary'.

with appropriate centralised risk evaluation, measure and control procedures.[207] In short, a group means a parent and subsidiaries that are subject to consolidated accounts.

For financial counterparties, an intragroup transaction means any one of the following four types of transactions specified in the EMIR:[208] for example, a financial counterparty (X) enters into an OTC derivative contract with another counterparty (Y) in the same group; X is established in the EU (or recognised by EU under EMIR art 13(2)) and Y is also a financial counterparty (including a financial holding company,[209] financial institution[210] or an undertaking offering ancillary services[211]); or a derivative contract is entered into with a non-financial counterparty that is part of the same group (subject to consolidation and central risk evaluation).[212]

In the U.S., the affiliate exemption is an extension of the end-user exemption. Under U.S. law, in principle, an 'affiliate' of an end-user may also qualify for the end-user exception, but only if the affiliate (acting on behalf of the end-user and as an agent) uses derivatives to hedge or mitigate the commercial risks of the end-user (or other affiliates of the same person that is not a financial entity and the manner in which it meets its financial obligations).[213] The CFTC clarifies that parties may elect not to clear a trade when a transaction is completed between a parent company and a subsidiary[214] or between two subsidiaries of the same parent firm.[215]

If a firm meets the above criteria, it is an 'eligible affiliate'.[216] The CFTC further clarifies that 'majority ownership interest' means holding a majority of equity shares, the right to receive upon dissolution or the contribution of the majority of capital of a partnership.[217] The affiliate exemption applies only if both counterparties elect not to clear the swap and if some conditions are met (e.g., the contract must be put in writing and subject to a centralised risk

---

207   EMIR art 3(1).
208   EMIR art 3(2).
209   A financial holding company is defined in EMIR art 2(18).
210   Under the EMIR, a 'financial institution' is a non-bank financial institution. EMIR art 2(17).
211   An 'ancillary services undertaking' is defined in EMIR art 2(19).
212   EMIR art 3(2)(d).
213   DFA s 723(a)(3), 7 USC 2(h)(7)(D)(i).
214   17 CFR 50.52(1)(a)(i) (2013).
215   17 CFR 50.52(1)(a)(ii) (2013).
216   17 CFR 50.52(2)(ii) (2013).
217   17 CFR 50.52 (2)(i) (2013).

management programme).²¹⁸ If an affiliate trades with an unaffiliated party, the affiliate must still comply with the clearing obligation where it applies.²¹⁹ No matter what, trades that qualify for the affiliate exception must still be reported to a trade repository.²²⁰ Nonetheless, the affiliate exception does not apply to the situations in which the affiliate is itself a swap dealer or major swap participant, an issuer defined in s 3 of the Investment Company Act,²²¹ a commodity pool or a bank holding company with over 5 billion of consolidated assets.²²²

In Singapore, the draft regulations in July 2015 did not propose an intra-group exemption. However, in Hong Kong, the clearing rules published in early 2016 provide that the clearing obligation does not apply to a person if the counterparty is an affiliate of the first person,²²³ provided that the affiliate's account is consolidated with the first party and that the first party gives an exemption notice to the regulator without cessation of the notice.²²⁴ In this regard, Hong Kong's approach is similar to that of the EU. It is not clear whether Singapore will pick up the intra-group exemption in the final rules.

4.4.4 Other Exemptions

Hong Kong provides a unique jurisdiction-based exemption that is not seen in Singapore. Pursuant to the clearing rules published in September 2016, the clearing obligation does not apply to a prescribed person if the counterparty to a trade is entered into in an exempt jurisdiction and the trade is recorded in the books of the prescribed person in that exempt jurisdiction, provided that the jurisdiction position in that exempt jurisdiction does not exceed 5% of the total position.²²⁵ To trigger this exemption, a prescribed person must also give notice to the regulator.²²⁶ The purpose of the jurisdiction exemption seems to address 'concerns about conflicting obligations that may apply to 'small' branches of a prescribed person operating in closed markets.'²²⁷ To ensure that it is 'small', the regulator sets the 5% limit accordingly.²²⁸ At this stage, it is not

---

218 17 CFR 50.52(b) (2013).
219 17 CFR 50.52(b)(4) (2013).
220 17 CFR 50.52(c) (2013).
221 15 USC 80a-3.
222 DFA s 723(a)(3), 7 USC 2(h)(7)(D)(ii).
223 HK Clearing Rules rule 8(1).
224 HK Clearing Rules rule 8(2) and (3).
225 HK Clearing Rules 9(1) and (2).
226 HK Clearing Rules 9(3) to (5).
227 HKSFC (n 113) at [112].
228 Id.

clear what the 'exempt jurisdictions' will be because this information is not provided in the latest consultation paper as in mid-2016.

In addition, Hong Kong will also allow for an exemption due to trade compression. The HKSFC recognises that trade compression is a common risk mitigation tool.[229] To allow firms to conduct trade compression to reduce overall exposure, the clearing rules provide that a trade is exempted if it is entered into by a person as a result of a multilateral portfolio compression cycle that meets the regulatory standards.[230] This exemption is also not yet available in Singapore.

4.5 Some Compliance Issues

4.5.1 Timing and Back-loading

How soon should a trade be sent to a CCP for clearing if it should be cleared? In Singapore, the proposed regulations in July 2015 require a trade to be cleared by a CCP within the same day that the trade is executed (or the next business day if that execution day is not a business day).[231] In Hong Kong, regulators plan to have the clearing on a T+1 basis, that is, the transaction must be cleared the day after the transaction date.[232] Thus, it is slightly more lenient in Hong Kong, although in practice it probably will not make much of a difference.

There are also back-loading issues for the clearing obligation. In Singapore, the draft regulations in July 2015 only require a specified derivative contract to be cleared if it is executed on or after the clearing commencement date.[233] In Hong Kong, a trade will be clearable if it is entered into after the implementation date of the clearing rules.[234] The rules or proposed rules in both markets mean that regulators do not require clearance of trades entered into before the commencement date of the clearing obligation, which should increase legal certainty for traders in the market.

4.5.2 Substituted Compliance

As with the reporting obligation, issues also exist regarding substituted compliance for the clearing obligation, such as a situation in which one or both parties are required to submit a trade for clearing if it is made between a Singaporean (or Hong Kong) bank and a U.S. bank. In Singapore, the law generally allows

---

229   HKSFC (n 113) at [114].
230   HK Clearing Rules 10(1) and (2).
231   Singapore Draft Clearing Rules reg 6(1).
232   HK Clearing Rules rule 6(1). HKSFC (n 113) [102].
233   Singapore Draft Clearing Rules reg 4(a).
234   HK Clearing Rules rule 6(1).

for substituted compliance of the clearing obligation in Singapore by clearance in a foreign CCP if the other party to a trade is a foreign person who is required to comply with the clearing requirements of that foreign country, provided that the foreign country in question is a 'relevant clearing jurisdiction'.[235] This allowance reflects the market reality in which the U.S. and the U.K. dominate the global derivatives market, which may make it impractical to force market participants to clear in a local CCP. Another concern is that forcing traders to clear in a local CCP may discourage some traders from trading or booking a transaction in Singapore, which in turn may hinder Singapore's ambition as an international financial centre. Moreover, if the main purpose of centralised clearing is to reduce counterparty and systemic risk, clearance in a foreign CCP serves the same purpose as long as the transaction is properly cleared. From the regulator's point of view, supervision of foreign cleared transactions could be controlled by the list of 'relevant foreign jurisdictions' and aided by international regulatory cooperation.[236]

However, the draft regulations published in July 2015 do not define 'relevant foreign jurisdictions'. Therefore, the possibility of substituted compliance under Singapore law is unclear until the MAS finalises the clearing rules. In Hong Kong, substituted compliance of the clearing obligation will be allowed under certain conditions. Under the draft clearing rules, a prescribed person is deemed to have complied with the clearing obligation if a trade is required to be cleared by the laws of a jurisdiction designated by the HKSFC and the trade is indeed cleared by a CCP in that jurisdiction with the CCP being a designated CCP.[237] Currently, Hong Kong's regulators seem to prefer to recognise member states of the OTC Derivatives Regulators Group[238] as 'comparable overseas jurisdictions'.[239] Its current members include most major markets, including the U.S., the EU, the U.K., Singapore, Hong Kong, Australia, Japan and South Korea; China is not yet a member of the organisation.[240]

---

235 SFA s 129F(1) (Singapore).
236 Monetary Authority of Singapore, 'Proposed Regulation of OTC Derivatives (P003–2012)' at 3.4.3, http://www.mas.gov.sg/News-and-Publications/Consultation-Paper/2012/Consultation-Paper-on-Proposed-Regulation-of-OTC-Derivatives.aspx.
237 HK Clearing Rules rule 11(1).
238 HKSFC (n 113) [117]-[120].
239 SFO Schedule 5, Part 2A, para 5.
240 See website of OTC Derivatives Regulators Forum: http://www.OTCdrf.org/about/members.htm.

Both Singapore and Hong Kong obtained recognition from the EU as 'equivalent' CCPs in 2014.²⁴¹ However, it seems that the Singapore Exchange is not referred to in the ESMA's public register as a recognised third-party CCP to clear some derivatives, whilst the Hong Kong Exchange (along with the Japan Securities Clearing Corporation) could conduct clearing businesses for European trades in June 2016.²⁴² It is certain that the Singapore Exchange will not sit idly, but how it will compete to get receive recognition from the ESMA remains to be seen.

4.5.3 Documentation Issues

Because the clearing obligation requires an OTC trade to be cleared by a CCP, this naturally means that the trade has to be transferred from an ISDA master agreement to be covered by a particular CCP. This necessarily raises some questions about documentation. Because the hallmark of the ISDA master agreement is its single-contract approach, centralised clearing means that some trades must be segregated from the otherwise 'single' contract to be cleared by a CCP. Whilst no universal documentation is applicable, the ISDA has collaborated with some other trade associations to create a template to facilitate centralised clearing of OTC derivatives. For example, we have seen the ISDA/FIA Cleared Derivatives Execution Agreement.²⁴³ It is not clear how Singapore and Hong Kong will cope with the documentation issue. It is most likely that both markets simply accept the market practices of the West for this purpose.

5 The Trading Mandate

The implementation of the trading mandate in Singapore and Hong Kong lags far behind the reporting and clearing mandate. As one of the three key mandates prescribed by the G20, the trading mandate was implemented in the U.S. in the DFA in 2010, section 2 of which provides that '[i]t shall be unlawful for any person, other than an eligible contract participant, to enter into a swap unless the swap is entered into on, or subject to the rules of, a board of

---

241 See EU website: http://ec.europa.eu/finance/financial-markets/derivatives/index_en .htm#maincontentSec4.
242 See ESMA publish registered as in 11 May 2016: https://www.esma.europa.eu/sites/default/ files/library/public_register_for_the_clearing_obligation_under_emir.pdf.
243 See https://www2.isda.org/emir/.

trade designated as a contract market....'.[244] The EU only responded in 2014 by prescribing the trading mandate in article 28 of the Markets in Financial Instruments Regulation, which requires derivatives listed in the register issued by the ESMA to be traded on an exchange.[245]

In Singapore, the amendment of the SFA in 2012 did not include the trading mandate. From the beginning, the MAS made it clear that it did not prefer to force mandatory exchange trading of derivatives in Singapore.[246] The MAS only signalled its intent to implement the trading mandate in early 2015 in a consultation paper.[247] However, as of May 2016, no further proposal has been made to amend the SFA in this regard, and no bill has yet been introduced into Parliament. Thus, it is still unclear how far and how long Singapore will implement the trading mandate.

In Hong Kong, the amendment of the SFO in 2014 provided a trading mandate.[248] S 101D provides that a prescribed person must execute an OTC derivative transaction that has been designated by regulators *only* on a designated trading platform in accordance with the trading rules issued by regulators.[249] In addition, if a prescribed person is an authorised financial institution (i.e., a bank), it must also ensure that a subsidiary specified by the HKMA must comply with the trade obligation if the subsidiary is a counterparty.[250] Like the clearing obligation, Hong Kong law also clarifies that a breach of the clearing obligation does not itself invalidate the transaction or affect the rights and obligations relating to the transaction.[251] In relation to the trading obligation, a 'prescribed person' means an authorised financial institution, an approved money broker, a licensed corporation or a person or class prescribed by the regulator.[252] Under the SFO, an 'authorised financial institution' (AI) means an authorised institution under s 2(1) of the Banking

---

244   DFA s 723(a), 7 USC 2(e).
245   Regulation (E.U.) No. 600/2014 art. 28 (MiFIR).
246   Above n 236, 23–24.
247   Monetary Authority of Singapore, 'Consultation Paper on Proposed Amendments to the Securities and Futures Act (P004–2015)', at 6, http://www.mas.gov.sg/News-and-Publications/Consultation-Paper/2015/Consultation-Paper-on-Proposed-Amendments-to-the-SFA.aspx.
248   SFO s 101D (Hong Kong).
249   SFO s 101D(1) (Hong Kong).
250   SFO s 101D(3) and (4) (Hong Kong).
251   SFO s 101C(6) (Hong Kong).
252   SFO s 101A (Hong Kong).

Ordinance (Cap 155),[253] which includes a bank, restricted license bank or deposit-taking company.[254] Thus, the term 'authorised financial institution' basically means banks and deposit-taking institutions. In addition, a 'licensed corporation' is defined in the SFO as 'a corporation which is granted a license under section 116 or 117 of [the SFO].'[255] In short, a licensed corporation means corporations (which may include partnerships or even sole proprietorships[256]) that hold a licence to carry on regulated activities in the SFO.[257] Nonetheless, it seems that insurance companies are not clearly covered by the definition of 'prescribed person' unless otherwise included by the HKMA and/or HKSFC.

However, the provision is not yet in effect as of May 2016, and the trading mandate has not yet been implemented in Hong Kong. Hong Kong's financial regulators have not yet issued any rule regarding the trading mandate as of May 2016. Thus, Hong Kong's position is not yet clear.

There are several possible explanations for the delayed implementation of the trading mandate. The first is market or economic factors. The success of mandatory exchange trading requires sufficient liquidity and trading volume. This is linked to the issue of substituted compliance. If substituted compliance is allowed, then the question is whether exchange operators in Hong Kong and Singapore could attract sufficient trades for a certain OTC derivative to be conducted in Asia rather than in more accomplished markets in the West. If, in contrast, substituted compliance is not allowed, the question then is whether a local exchange would attract sufficient trades to offset opposing transactions. Otherwise, the risk to an exchange and the market might be higher. Either way, Singapore and Hong Kong must compete with American and European giants for a share of the pie in a market dominated by Western banks as major dealers, even in the era of electronic trading.

The second possible explanation may be market infrastructure. In both Hong Kong and Singapore, there are proper futures exchanges (e.g., the Hong Kong Exchange or Singapore Exchange) that are comparable with the 'contract market' in the U.S. and the 'regulated market' in the EU. However, neither Singapore nor Hong Kong has adopted the ideas of a 'swap execution facility'[258] in the U.S. or an 'organised trading facility'[259] in the EU. This might affect the

---

253 SFO Schedule 1 (Hong Kong).
254 Banking Ordinance s 2(1) (Hong Kong).
255 SFO Schedule 1 (Hong Kong).
256 SFO Schedule 10 paragraphs 27–30 (Hong Kong).
257 See SFO ss 116 and 117 (Hong Kong).
258 1 USC 1a(50).
259 MiFIR art. 2(1)(15).

future implementation of the trading mandate. Because no clear regulatory intent has been declared at the time of writing, we must wait and see how it is developed in the future.

6 Convergence, Divergence or a Room for Arbitrage? An Evaluation of Positions in Hong Kong and Singapore

Based on the discussion above, what can we learn from the development of OTC derivatives in Hong Kong and Singapore in relation to the powerful markets in U.S. and Europe? Does greater convergence of the regulations exist due to the works of international soft law and TRNs? Or should we expect greater regulatory competition to acquire business in the post-Lehman era? If the answer to the latter question is negative, we probably should expect to see some regulatory arbitrage in the future.

By comparing the current rules in Hong Kong and Singapore, we observe that the reporting mandate is generally well accepted in both markets. Not only has the reporting mandate been implemented first, but the substance of their reporting obligations is generally in line with each other and with those in the U.S. or the EU. Although some technical differences still exist, we suggest that those differences are not huge. A higher degree of convergence regarding the reporting mandate may exist partly because the main rationale behind trade reporting is to improve transparency, a common goal to all regulators. The critical question then becomes how to acquire and/or share information. The most critical difference may be regarding substituted compliance, whereby Hong Kong seems to prefer local reporting whilst Singapore is more accommodating to substituted compliance. Whether the differences may cause some shift in the trading activities in Asia or globally may require further empirical studies.

Second, the delay in the implementation of the clearing and trading mandates in Hong Kong and Singapore may reflect conflicting driving forces behind the migration of financial regulatory norms. The global financial crisis was obviously the intervening event that triggered the regulatory reforms. However, the crisis mainly affected financial institutions in the U.S., U.K. and EU, which explains why regulators in key Western markets are more keen to implement the clearing mandate to improve market stability. However, conflicting concerns face Asian regulators. On the one hand, both markets and CCPs would certainly have an interest in competing for clearing businesses from the West. For this purpose, there is a force to push Asian regulators to implement the clearing mandate, in addition to pressure from major markets or international organisations. On the other hand, the effectiveness of the clearing mandate is built upon the solvency of a CCP and the clearing system. With Western traders still dominating the market amid the rise of electronic trading,[260] Asian regulators face the dilemma to either accept substituted compliance (with the potential effect that some clearing business might head to more established Western CCPs and thereby reduce liquidity) or to force local clearing (with the risk of losing business completely to other CCPs around the world). This underlines the challenges that face regulators in Singapore and Hong Kong and may offer an explanation to the lengthy delay in its implementation. In other words, the trading volume in Singapore and Hong Kong may not fully justify the costs of mandatory clearing. Those factors may also explain why Singapore and Hong Kong differ in certain regards, such as the exemptions to mandatory clearing. Regarding the trading mandate, the delay is even more obvious, for the reasons illustrated above.[261]

In the end, does any possibility of a 'race to the bottom' exist? We argue that this possibility is low for many reasons. For example, an American bank cannot discharge its clearing obligation under U.S. law by clearing in any CCP outside the U.S. There is a concern in the U.S. and the EU to prevent their traders from circumventing American or European regulations. Because major derivatives dealers are mostly in the West, American or European regulations should have an effect on controlling Western traders from arbitraging any leniency in regulations outside the U.S. or the EU. In addition, to gain clearing or trading businesses from Western traders, Singapore and Hong Kong might have some incentives to implement global reforms and to make regulations coherent with the U.S. and/or EU. In other words, the market should have its effect of reducing significant regulatory arbitrage.

---

260   Many OTC derivatives were executed electronically. According to the International Organization of Securities Commissions, as in June 2010, about 12.3% of OTC interest rate swaps were executed electronically (16.7% for credit derivatives and 14.3% for equity derivatives). Technical Committee of the International Organization of Securities Commissioners, *Report on Trading of OTC Derivatives* (FR03/11, February 2011) 8 in https://www.iosco.org/library/pubdocs/pdf/IOSCOPD345.pdf. The ISDA has also developed 'Financial products Markup Language (FpML) to facilitate electronic dealing and processing. See ISDA website: https://www2.isda.org/functional-areas/technology-infrastructure/fpml/.

261   See *supra* Part v.

7 Conclusions

In conclusion, this article seeks to examine the current development of OTC derivatives regulations in Singapore and Hong Kong by examining various issues, from regulatory scope and definition issues to key issues regarding the three main mandates: reporting, clearing and trading mandates. For each mandate, we examine the rationale, legal foundation and jurisdiction scope, the parties and transactions subject to the mandates and certain compliance issues including timing, back-loading and substituted compliance. In general, we observe that the reporting mandate is generally well received in Singapore and Hong Kong. Whilst some technical differences exist, both markets have adopted similar legal structures and rules in comparison with U.S. and EU regulations. We have seen a long delay in the implementation of the clearing mandate, although it seems that both markets intend to implement the clearing mandate by late 2016. There is even further delay regarding the trading mandate, with no implementation time table in sight. The delay may be partly due to market realities and concerns surrounding the solvency of the clearing systems. Even comparing draft clearing rules, we have seen some differences between the two markets (e.g., exemptions to the clearing mandate). Whether those differences might result in a shift of trading activities or a regulatory competition to or from Asia and whether those reforms have reduced systemic risk and market efficiency will be issues worth monitoring in the future.

Bibliography

Avgouleas, Emilios. 2012. *Governance of Global Financial Markets: The Law, The Economics, The Politics*. Cambridge University Press.

Awrey, Dan. 2010. "The Dynamics of OTC Derivatives Regulation: Bridging the Public-Private Divide." *European Business Organization Law Review* 11 (2). 2010: 155–93.

Braithwaite, Joanne P. 2011. "The Inherent Limits of 'Legal Devices': Lessons for the Public Sector's Central Counterparty Prescription for the OTC Derivatives Markets." *European Business Organisation Law Review* 12 (1). 2011: 87–119.

Brummer, Chris. 2012. *Soft Law and the Global Financial System: Rule Making in the 21st Century*. Cambridge: Cambridge University Press.

Chamorro-Courtland, Christian. 2012. "The Trillion Dollar Question: Can A Central Bank Bail Out A Central Counterparty Clearing House Which Is 'Too Big to Fail'?" *Brook J Corp Fin & Com L* 6: 433.

Chen, Christopher. 2014. "Measuring the Transplantation of English Commercial Law in a Small Jurisdiction: An Empirical Study of Singapore's Insurance Judgments between 1965 and 2012." *Texas International Law Journal* 49 (3): 469–505.

Cho, Sungjoon, and Claire R. Kelly. 2012. "Promises and Perils of New Global Governance: A Case of the G20." *Chicago Journal International Law* 12: 491–562.

Cohen, Saul S. 1995. "Financial Services Regulation: A Mid-Decade Review: Colloquium: The Challenge of Derivatives." *Fordham L Rev* 63. 1995: 1993.

Financial Stability Board. 2010. "Implementing OTC Derivatives Market Reforms." http://www.financialstabilityboard.org/wp-content/uploads/r_101025.pdf.

Financial Stability Board. 2011. "OTC Derivatives Market Reforms – Progress Report on Implementation." http://www.financialstabilityboard.org/wp-content/uploads/r_110415b.pdf.

Financial Stability Board. 2014. "Key Attributes of Effective Resolution Regimes for Financial Institutions." http://www.financialstabilityboard.org/2014/10/r_141015/.

Flanagan, Sean M. 2001. "The Rise of a Trade Association: Group Interactions within the International Swaps and Derivatives Association." *Harvard Negotiation Law Review* 6: 211–63.

Gadinis, Stavros. 2015. "Three Pathways to Global Standards: Private, Regulator, and Ministry Network." *American Journal of International Law* 109: 1–57.

Galbraith, Jean, and David Zaring. 2014. "Soft Law as Foreign Relations Law." *Cornell Law Review* 99: 735–94.

Griffith, Sean J. 2014. "Substituted Compliance and Systemic Risk: How to Make a Global Market in Derivative Regulation." *Minnesota Law Review* 98: 1291–1373.

Henderson, Schuyler K. 2010. *Henderson on Derivatives*. 2nd Ed. London: LexisNexis.

Hong Kong Monetary Authority. 2015. "Frequently Asked Questions on the Securities and Future (OTC Derivative Transactions—Reporting and Record Keeping Obligations) Rules." Hong Kong. http://www.hkma.gov.hk/media/eng/doc/key-information/guidelines-and-circular/2015/20150710e1.pdf.

Hong Kong Securities and Futures Commission. 2011. "Consultation Paper on the Proposed Regulatory Regime for the Over-the-Counter Derivatives Market in Hong Kong." Hong Kong. http://www.sfc.hk/edistributionWeb/gateway/EN/consultation/doc?refNo=11CP6.

Hong Kong Securities and Futures Commission. 2012. "Joint Consultation Conclusions on the Proposed Regulatory Regime for the Over-the-Counter Derivatives Market in Hong Kong." Hong Kong. http://www.sfc.hk/edistributionWeb/gateway/EN/consultation/conclusion?refNo=11CP6.

Hong Kong Securities and Futures Commission. 2012. "Supplement Consultation on the OTC Derivatives Regime for Hong Kong—Proposed Scope of New/Expanded Regulated Activities and Regulatory Oversight of Systemically Important Players."

Hong Kong. http://www.sfc.hk/edistributionWeb/gateway/EN/consultation/doc?refNo=12CP2.

Hong Kong Securities and Futures Commission. 2016. "Consultation Conclusions and Further Consultation on Introducing Mandatory Clearing and Expanding Mandatory Reporting." Hong Kong. http://www.sfc.hk/edistributionWeb/gateway/EN/consultation/doc?refNo=16CP1.

Hong Kong Securities and Futures Commission. 2013. "Consultation Conclusions and Further Consultation on the Securities and Futures (OTC Derivative Transactions—Reporting and Record Keeping Obligations) Rules." Hong Kong. http://www.sfc.hk/edistributionWeb/gateway/EN/consultation/doc?refNo=14CP8.

Kanda, Hideki, and Curtis J Milhaupt. 2003. "Re-Examining Legal Transplants: The Director's Fiduciary Duty in Japanese Corporate Law." *American Journal of Comparative Law* 51. 2003: 887–901.

Kress, Jeremy C. 2011. "Credit Default Swaps, Clearinghouses, and Systemic Risk: What Centralised Counterparties Must Have Access to Central Bank Liquidity?" *Harv J on Legis* 48. 2011: 49–93.

Le Vine, Barry. 2011. "The Derivative Market's Black Sheep: Regulation of Non-Cleared Security-Based Swap under Dodd-Frank." *Northwestern Journal of International Law and Business* 31. 2011: 699–737.

Manns, Jeffrey. 2013. "Insuring against a Derivative Disaster: The Case for Decentralised Risk Management." *Iowa Law Review* 98: 1575–1627.

Monetary Authority of Singapore. 2012. "Proposed Regulation of OTC Derivatives (P003–2012)." Singapore. http://www.mas.gov.sg/News-and-Publications/Consultation-Paper/2012/Consultation-Paper-on-Proposed-Regulation-of-OTC-Derivatives.aspx.

Monetary Authority of Singapore. 2012. "Consultation Paper I on Proposed Amendments to the Securities and Futures Act on Regulation of OTC Derivatives (P008–2012)." Singapore. http://www.mas.gov.sg/News-and-Publications/Consultation-Paper/2012/Consultation-Paper-I-on-Proposed-Amendments-to-the-SFA-on-Regulation-of-OTC-Derivatives.aspx.

Monetary Authority of Singapore. 2015. "Draft Regulations for Mandatory Clearing of Derivatives Contracts (P010–2015)." Singapore. http://www.mas.gov.sg/News-and-Publications/Consultation-Paper/2015/Consultation-Paper-on-Draft-Regulations-for-Mandatory-Clearing-of-Derivatives-Contracts.aspx.

Monetary Authority of Singapore. 2015. "Consultation Paper on Proposed Amendments to the Securities and Futures Act (P004–2015)." Singapore. http://www.mas.gov.sg/News-and-Publications/Consultation-Paper/2015/Consultation-Paper-on-Proposed-Amendments-to-the-SFA.aspx.

Monetary Authority of Singapore. 2016. "Proposed Amendments to the Securities & Futures (Reporting of Derivatives Contracts) Regulations (P002–2016)." Singapore.

http://www.mas.gov.sg/News-and-Publications/Consultation-Paper/2016/Consultation-Paper-on-Proposed-Amendments-to-the-SF-Reporting-of-Derivatives-Contracts-Regulations.aspx.

Nichol, Andrew. 2013. "Hedging against the Next Financial Crisis: Proposals for Managing Systemic Risk in Centrally Cleared Derivatives Transactions." *Banking and Finance Law Review* 29: 169–84.

Nichols, Cheryl. 2008. "Mutual Recognition Based on Substituted Compliance: An Integral Component of the SEC's Mandate." *NC J Int'l L & Com Reg 1* 34. 2008: 1–109.

Pirrong, Craig. 2011. "The Economics of Central Clearing: Theory and Practice." ISDA. http://www2.isda.org/news/isda-publishes-the-economics-of-central-clearing-theory-and-practice-a-discussion-paper-on-clearing-issues.

Roe, Mark J. 2013. "Clearinghouse Overconfidence." *Cal. L. Rev.* 101: 1641–1703.

Verdier, Pierre-Hugues. 2013. "The Political Economy of International Financial Regulation." *Indiana Law Journal* 88: 1405–74.

Wendt, Froukelien. 2015. "Central Counterparties: Addressing Their Too Important to Fail Nature." WP/15/21. https://www.imf.org/external/pubs/ft/wp/2015/wp1521.pdf.

Yadav, Yesha. 2013. "The Problematic Case of Clearinghouses in Complex Markets." *Georgetown L. J.* 101: 387–444.

Printed in the United States
By Bookmasters